Mesearch and the Performing Body

Mark Edward

Mesearch and the Performing Body

palgrave
macmillan

Mark Edward
Department of Performing Arts
Edge Hill University
Ormskirk, UK

ISBN 978-3-319-69997-4   ISBN 978-3-319-69998-1   (eBook)
https://doi.org/10.1007/978-3-319-69998-1

Library of Congress Control Number: 2017960872

Cover illustration: Détail de la Tour Eiffel © nemesis2207/Fotolia.co.uk

Printed on acid-free paper

This Palgrave Pivot imprint is published by Springer Nature
The registered company is Springer International Publishing AG
The registered company address is: Gewerbestrasse 11, 6330 Cham, Switzerland

Dedicated to the memory of my lovely sister Denise, who enjoyed laughing, dancing and talking (quite a lot) and Mylo for his loyal friendship.

ACKNOWLEDGEMENTS

I would like to say thank you to Dr Fiona Bannon and Dr George Rodosthenous for their supervision of my PhD entitled: *Temporality of the Performing Body: Movement, Memory, Mesearch,* which has contributed towards the writing of this book. I would also like to thank Professor Simon Piasecki and Simon Lewandowski for their encouraging feedback and positivity during my PhD viva. Equally, I offer my sincerest gratitude to my editors Vicky Peters and Vicky Bates at Palgrave, to the production team at Springer, and my indexer, Judith Lavender.

Being a collaborative artist and academic, there are many other people to whom I need to offer in thanks in the realisation of the projects discussed in this book. I am most grateful to Peter Bennett, Chris D' Bray, Rosa Fong, Dr Mark Fremaux, Julia Griffin, Dr Karen Lauke, Olivia du Monceau and Professor Helen Newall.

I am grateful to Mel Gibbons for providing photos of June Sands and the photographers Shane Green, Olivia du Monceau, Professor Helen Newall and Stuart Rayner for their kind permission of use throughout this practice-led volume.

I would like to say thank you to both Edge Hill University for their support in the research process and to the peer reviewers for their helpful suggestions. I would also like to say thank you to my mother (Sylvia) and my father (Joe), as well as my sisters (Val and Liz) for their love and encouragement throughout my life. I am appreciative to all my current and former students who have helped me to mature as an educator and taught me the act of patience.

I am grateful to Naked Acts: Flesh and Queer Symposium (2017), Manchester Drag Symposium (2017), Talking Bodies conference (2015), TaPRA Performer Training Working Group (2014), IFTR Queer Futures Working Group (2013), Sadler's Wells Art of Age conference (2014), Bank Street Art Gallery, Homotopia (2012) Festival and Making Sense of Pain conference (2011) for allowing me to disseminate and discuss my ongoing research.

I want to express gratitude to my civil partner, Dr Chris Greenough, who has wiped away the many tears from my extremely tired eyes and helped to keep me borderline sane through his sensitivity coupled with his academic and emotionally intelligent feedback.

Finally, I want to say thank you to the many quirky and extraordinary people who have found their way to me throughout life. This array of people who have shared their cultures, wisdom, honesty, ideas, laughter, tears and most of all their wonderful performing experiences.

CONTENTS

LIST OF FIGURES

CHAPTER 1

From Stage to Page: Introducing Me

Abstract In this chapter, I set out my personal subjective position as a dance maker and the professional reasons which led to my corpus of work around ageing performers. With a focus on how ageing is understood, experienced and reflected upon I explore a personal context into the subjectivity of dancing identity, embodiment, transformation of the bodily agent and an archiving of the body. The chapter sets out the main themes which are discussed in the book: How do mature artists explore age(ing) and embodiment as a cultural and social construct through my practice? Can performers engage with reflective methodologies when creating performance and how is this documented? How do dancing performers' bodies negotiate and renegotiate age(ing) in performance?

Keywords Artist • Performer • Self • Contemporary dance • Research • Ageing

My practical and written work explores my own ageing and non-heterosexual identities in dance and performance. Here, adopting an entirely appropriate analogy, I offer what Nancy Miller terms 'the obligatory dance cards of representivity' in which the author dances 'the waltz of the *as a...*' (1991: 121; my emphasis) where the author fills the ellipses with one's markers of identity of choice. *As an* interdisciplinary

© The Author(s) 2018
M. Edward, *Mesearch and the Performing Body*,
https://doi.org/10.1007/978-3-319-69998-1_1

1

artist/performer, my work explores and challenges notions of (my) age-ing and counters the notion of 'normative' bodies. I use the term 'artist' and 'performer' now, when I used to call myself a 'dancer'. With a back-ground in live art and both contemporary[1] and western classical dance, I pursued both undergraduate and postgraduate studies in these areas, before embarking on my own career in performance arts education, as an academic in dance and performance art. To be truthful, the term 'dancer' began to sit uncomfortably with me when my practice output was studio based with my students, as a number of years had passed since I was involved in 'professional' dance work. Equally, the wider scope of performance studies enabled me to recognise the interdisciplinary nature of my creative output. Within this introduction, I would like to identify the frames of 'dance' to which I make reference throughout this book. My use of the term 'dance' acknowledges it as an art and a discipline; its performative form. Aside from being performance based, I appreciate dance as recreational, such as community dance and the emergence of healing dance therapies such as somatic practices and dance movement therapy (DMT). Yet, my reference to 'dance' as a noun in this book, because of the issues of age and representivity which underpin my work, refers to dance in its performance form.

My performance research interests have been driven by experiences of ageing resulting in three main questions. These questions, which are answered throughout the course of the text, are informed by the idea of explaining and exploring the dynamics of creative performance making in the context of my life trajectory. With a focus on how (self) ageing is understood, experienced and reflected upon, I use my personal context to explore subjectivities in relation to myself as an ageing performer. These themes include identity, embodiment, transformation of the bodily agent and an archiving of the body. In positing these lines of explorations within the book, the questions below are interwoven as follows:

- How do I, as a mature artist, explore age(ing) and embodiment as a cultural and social construct through my practice?
- How do I, as a performer, engage with reflective methodologies when creating performance and how does the documentation form part of my practice?
- How does my (maturing) dancing performers' body negotiate and renegotiate age(ing) in performance?

Following this introduction, Chap. 2 provides a literature review of both emic and etic literature in the interdisciplinary areas of sociology, performance studies and identity theories. Chapter 3 frames the current position of performance-based studies into ageing and performance, with a review of practitioners and performance work. For me, my research actually emerges from my professional practice, therefore I use the term practice-led to describe my working methods. In such a context, the choice of autobiographical practice-led research is one of the main methods I used to generate and analyse performance in relation to theoretical investigations. It is within Chap. 4 that my original mode of inquiry, built on the foundation of autobiography and autoethnography is discussed, using what I denote as a more accessible term 'mesearch'.[2] The work then explores three practice-led works: *Falling Apart at the Seams, Council House Movie Star* and *Dying Swans and Dragged Up Dames*. In referring to my practice-led work, I offer reflections of the practice, photographs and underpinning academic sources that are offered for the reader. My practice chapters (Chaps. 5, 6 and 7) focus explicitly on engagement with reflexive methodologies and the documentation of my process, yet each one also looks at the negotiation of age through both social and physical lenses, yet which are personal to myself. Finally, Chap. 8 offers some closing reflections on mesearch and the need for such subjective explorative inquiries.

Although the practice work itself aims to demonstrate its own coherence and intellectual rigour, this book provides the academic and scholarly context of the research projects. This book merges and glues together my practice in terms of exploring my archived documentation, critical reflections, writings and visual material. Originally seeds were sown in my doctoral thesis, yet my research has also seen the germination of ongoing theorising and ideas set out in my previous publications in the following areas: mental illness, identity and dance (Edward with Bannon 2017), mesearch and risky ethics (Edward 2018), mesearch and ethics in doing self and sexuality in performance (Edward and Farrier forthcoming), queering and que(e)rying the site and body through drag costume (Edward 2014a) and autoethnographical and ethnographical research into dancing negativity among boys who engage in dance (Edward 2014b).

This text seeks to provide a distinct contribution to knowledge in the areas of practice-led research, self-reflexivity, self-ageing and performance, in which I offer my own experiences and reflections as self-as-practice to detail my engagement with performance and ageing. This text is offered as a unique self-study discussing the impact of ageing in dance and performance, and I am both author and content of the investigation. The research seeks to provide a space where I, as a performer, renegotiate the process of ageing, and I seek to value my new embodiment in its maturing performing form. So, instead of claiming to explore solely a personal paradigm, I explore what Boud and Griffin term as a 'new paradigm' (1987: 113). In light of this 'new paradigm' I explore the possibilities of performance beyond the culture backdrop of dancing youthful elitism that appears to discriminate against getting older, which is ripe for original, distinctive, unique and creative possibilities for performance.

NOTES

1. Before my formal training in contemporary dance and ballet I was part of the 1988 UK acid house movement where I engaged in dancing at illegal raves, consuming recreational drugs and developed a 'fuck you' attitude towards a Thatcherist society. This 1980s raving period allowed me to understand who I was becoming (through a sense of self-discovery) during my teenage years as a young gay man living in the northern working-class community of Shevington, near Wigan. For further reading see Edward, M. (2015) 'Dance: Anarchy from the Margins and Free Expression' in Gillieron, R. and Robson, C. (Eds.) *Counter Culture UK: A Celebration*. Twickenham: Supernova Books. http://supernovabooks.co.uk/products-page/.
2. See Emma Rees's article in https://www.timeshighereducation.com/features/self-reflective-study-the-rise-of-mesearch/2019097.article. Mesearch is a term which has been adopted from my doctoral thesis. That said, I would not claim to have coined a new term, but it is unique to me in describing my creative and autoexplorative methodologies in performance.

BIBLIOGRAPHY

Boud, D. and Griffin, V. (1987) *Appreciating Adults Learning: From the Learners' Perspective*. London: Kogan Page.

Edward, M. (2014a) 'Council House Movie Star: Que(e)rying the Costume'. Special issue in *Scene*, 2: 1+2, pp. 147–153, https://doi.org/10.1386/scene.7.1-7.147_1

Edward, M. (2014b) 'Stop Prancing About: Boys, Dance and the Reflective Glance'. Special issue in *Men Doing (In)Equalities Research*, 470–479. Emerald Group Publishing Limited.

Edward, M. (2018) 'Between Dance and Detention: Ethical Considerations of Mesearch in Performance' in Iphofen, R. and Tolech, M. (Eds.) *The Sage Handbook of Ethics in Qualitative Research*. Sage.

Edward, M. with Bannon, F. (2017) 'Being in Pieces: Integrating Dance, Identity and Mental Health' in Karkou, V., Oliver, S. and Lycouris, S. (Eds.) *The Oxford Handbook of Dance and Wellbeing*. New York: Oxford University Press.

Edward, M. and Farrier, S. (forthcoming) 'Doing Me: Researching as Me-searching. Ruminations on Research Methodology in Drag Performance' in Claes, T., Porrovecchio, A. and Reynolds, P. (Eds.) *Methodological and Ethical Issues in Sex and Sexuality Research: Contemporary Essays*. Barbara Buldrich Publishers, Lerverkusen, Germany.

Miller, N. (1991) *Getting Personal: Feminist Occasions and Other Autobiographical Acts*. London: Routledge.

CHAPTER 2

Declining Dancers

Abstract This chapter offers consideration of how the development of a dancer/performer's identity is linked to one's personal identity. Subsequently, I then tackle wider issues of identity, underpinned by sociological scholarship in relation to a subjective turn within research. Ageing and dance in western cultural studies are only recently becoming emerging areas of scholarship. In light of this, my range is interdisciplinary, including sociological texts as a framework to explore identity, ageing and autoethnography. I highlight the lack of visibility of ageing performers.

Keywords Ageing dancers • Biographies • Choreographer • Sociology • Autoethnography • Identity

This chapter contextualises existent research on ageing in dance alongside pertinent themes found in studies on identity. The theme of identity is essential to my methodological principle of mesearch. The emergence of this subjective paradigm offers a platform to explore my individualised experiences of dance and ageing, which is entirely relevant to my performance works. Accordingly, this chapter reviews the existent framework of scholarship in relation to dance and ageing which is relevant to my own position as an ageing artist. The first section offers a brief exploration of how the development of a dancer/performer iden-

© The Author(s) 2018   7
M. Edward, *Mesearch and the Performing Body*,
https://doi.org/10.1007/978-3-319-69998-1_2

tity is linked to one's personal identity. Subsequently, the second part of my discussion explores wider issues of identity, underpinned by sociological scholarship in relation to a turn to self within research. The interdisciplinary range, to include sociological texts as a framework to explore identity, ageing and autoethnography, autobiography and narratives of self, is largely due to the fact that literature on ageing and dance in western cultural studies are only recently becoming emerging areas of scholarship.

DANCE AND THE AGE AGENDA

> Some dancers, like Nureyev and Fonteyn, may be able to dance until they are quite old: audiences attracted by their fame will forgive their declining technique, and choreographers will tailor rules to suit their dwindling abilities. Most dancers are not so indulged. The majority are forced to quit far earlier. Their bodies simply give out. (Lee 1989: 27)

In agreement with Lee, I observe how the tone and words here actually reinforce the situation rather than observe a phenomenon. Ageing dancers have rarely had viewership, and those who have continued their careers past the 'dance by date' are able to do so based on their previous success and fame. Sadly, the themes of declining abilities and sorrow for the youthful former self have become an overt caricature for ageing dance artists. Thus, there is a narrow frame in what is perceived to be classified as 'dance' practice, in which choreography and technical prowess are youth-driven. There exist two main forms of ageing: chronological ageing and physical ageing, and these distinctions are significant when we look at the lifespan of a dancer's career. Clive Barnes, when he was writing in the *New York Times*, notes that:

> A dancer's career can be seen, in its simplest form, as two graph lines. The first is an ascending curve of a dancer's artistry, the second is a descending curve of his physical condition. Where these two lines intersect is the peak of a career. After this peak, the dancer's artistry usually continues to increase, but his physical losses outbalance the increase. (cited in Lee 1989: 27)

Adopting Barnes's two-line approach, I offer a cross-section line to the discussion. This additional line needs to demonstrate the possibilities of renegotiating bodily mechanics, and how this renegotiation can offer more suitable forms of dance. This renegotiation can work by adapting previous repertoire or dance techniques to suit the ability of the maturing mover. Simply, that the artistry and ability can both be reshaped. As one ages, there is an increase in one's expertise as a choreographer and human-container of embodied forms and techniques. Yet, there is a decrease in marketability, as the ageing dancer's visibility is limited in terms of performance opportunities.

To begin my discussion of ageing in dance and before tackling the emic literature, I offer my own reflection of the intersection of my artistry and physical condition. In 2013 I presented my reflections as an arts practitioner in dance and growing older in a co-written paper *Not With My Body Ya Don't! Ageing Dancers and the Habitus Turn* delivered at the Theatre and Performance Research Association (TaPRA) conference in Glasgow. Below is an excerpt in which I reflect on my career in dance from 1995 up until 2013, acknowledging how my notion of embodiment has changed in this period through consideration of older performers:

> In 1995, and as a much younger dance artist, I was fortunate enough to watch (the then 59-year-old) postmodern dancer Trisha Brown perform her work *If You Couldn't See Me*, a solo in which Brown had her back to the audience throughout the whole of her performance. The only visibility was the musculature and skin on her back, which she rippled and folded. She was framed not only by the rich gilt proscenium arch of the Blackpool Grand Theatre but also by dance pieces before and after this piece performed by her company of dancers much younger than herself. I was mesmerised by this older dancer and the rippling of her skin and the movement of her breath. Her hair was loose and greying. She was not pretending to be anything other than she was. And it was beautiful. But as Brown intensified her dancing, a friend of mine leaned over and whispered in my ear: 'The reason she won't show her face is because she's an old bag and really shouldn't be dancing.' At the time, I was not angry on Brown's behalf, in fact, I laughed, but I was confused, because this was a signal that I should not find this beautiful. And the payback is that I feel I have since become the dancer that maybe considered 'an old bag who really shouldn't be dancing'. And now, if I could watch that piece again, I would totally sympathise: I would not objectify her performing body in terms of technique, and how it is worn like a strait-jacket by the body. Now, I would see the living archive in a body that has danced beyond technique and which now performs itself. I wish my younger self could have understood this. (Edward and Newall 2013: 7)

My research into negotiating age as a performer and developing an understanding of the value of age is at the core of my ongoing performance-based work. Recent research has been conducted in the area of dance and the ageing body (Amans 2013; Schwaiger 2012), ageing and everyday life (Thomas 2013), ageing bodies in culture (Hepworth 2003), images of ageing (Featherstone and Wernick 1995), as well as a range of community based and creative performance, such as the UK-based projects for Company of Elders and Liz Lerman's USA-based Dancers of the Third Age.[1] Thus, the process of my research engages in investigations that attempt to revisit, revise and renegotiate the body through shifts in habitual patterns of dance and performance genealogy, alongside a cultural and sociological 'turn' in visibility and expectation. My introductory journey through dance and ageing is informed by scholarship from eminent dance scholars, such as Justine Coupland and Gwyn (2003), Justine Coupland (2013), Helen Thomas (2013) and social and cultural theorists, Featherstone et al. (1991) and Marguerite Gullette (1999). Within Chap. 3, I explore artists who engage with dance and ageing from practitioner perspectives.

Coupland notes 'our bodies are old, we are not. Old age is thus understood as a state in which the body is in opposition to the self. We are alienated from our bodies' (Coupland and Gwyn 2003: 5). Whereas the mind will contain the narrative and memory of the body, the body itself comes under scrutiny for critique. As Gullette states, an engagement with self-narratives of ageing and dance allows one to 'reconnect with one's distinctive life story and unique subjectivity' (1999: 55).

Featherstone, Hepworth and Turner's research highlighted how the portrayal of ageing by the media and advertising has resulted in a policing of ageing skin. Their work interrogates images of positive ageing in the 1960s and 1970s within the *Retirement Choice* magazine (1991), claiming that what is described as 'middle aged' should be extended, as people are not considered to enter their third age for much longer. This is partly due to anti-ageing methods as well as lifestyle choices. In one example, the editorial expresses the distinction between ageing and retirement: 'Isn't it about time the news got around that nowadays people stay younger and are not old in the same way that people were old in the time of yore?' (Featherstone et al. 1991: 37). Conway and Hockey (1998) have explored how the use of cosmetics, clothing and surgery are being used by people to resist the 'mask of ageing'. In 2004, Hepworth pluralised the term 'masks of ageing' to include the notion of society as an embodied agency. In terms of dance, Schwaiger (2009) has argued for the visibility of the gendered ageing performer within theatrical productions, seeking to recognise the cultural value of mature gendered female dancers.

Due to social and cultural influences including the media, it becomes apparent that mainstream conservative western[2] dance also boldly moves us to a body normative. This includes the removing of individual expressions, an absence of fat visibility[3] and an eradication of visual signs of physical ageing, such as facial lines. This serves to control, monitor and police the matured body. Thomas agrees, 'there is a gap between the recognition of the outward physical appearance of the ageing body' (Thomas 2013: 110). Thomas develops the visual presence of ageing, following Featherstone, Hepworth and Turner, who argue that:

> The perceived signs of ageing are not individual, but are part and parcel of a restrictive discourse of ageing which, as Featherstone and Hepworth (1991) argue, impedes the possibilities for different modes of self-expression. (Thomas 2013: 112)

In the context of professional dance, unspoken age discrimination is witnessed by an absence of range on the stage. The training process is intense and dancing ideals are set up as goals in terms of physical aesthetics. What ensues is a relatively short career-span for the professional dance artist. Such idealised notions of physicality in dance leads to a body commodity, and this is highlighted through the preference for artists who remain youthful, strong, muscular and physically vibrant.[4]

Ultimately, as I have observed over my career in the dance industry and the academy, there is a migration for ageing artists into teaching, mentoring and choreography. Obviously, one reason for this is that dance, as a physical act, is more taxing on the muscle and bones, yet the migration does acknowledge that the older artist is still mentally capable of creating work for performance. There is a wealth in experience in terms of dissemination of practice, which leads to renewal and thereby expands the discipline. Not only are dancers restricted by the physical effects of ageing, the personal journey is further compounded by no longer experiencing the thrill and joy of their youthful performances. Their enhanced understanding of dance and choreography moves from the physical to the theoretical. A similar position occurs within sporting and athletic maturing bodies (see Phoenix and Sparkes 2008; Sparkes 2009). Andrew Sparkes's work explores how embodiment, life history and autoethnography can combine to trace the trajectory by which the body changes over time. His thesis is that sporting embodiment can be experienced in different ways by the same person in different contexts. Sparkes also explores the relationship and dialogue between the body, self and culture. Similar work is needed to look into this migration within dance communities, as the brutal impact of ageing on individual life courses in dance remains underexplored. Yet, the parallels between ageing in dance and ageing in sport are more nuanced, as Lee reminds us:

> Fame and the ageing dancer cannot be compared to fame and the aging athlete. Dancers are not used to inspire advertising campaigns after their retirement, nor do they achieve the levels of salary or benefits of athletes. (1989: 30)

I suspect Lee's assertion from the late 1980s is correct in terms of salary and benefits, yet within Chap. 3 I discuss the work of Alexander Ferri, who has embraced her identity as an ageing dancer to advertise anti-ageing products in the United Kingdom. Nonetheless, older bodies in dance have much to offer as a valued archive, but like all archives, they wait, gathering dust, for an interested party to discover and appreciate them. Their existence is an important resource which demonstrates a phenomenology of the body that has the marks of time, of life experiences and emotions alongside a wealth of performance techniques that can still be culturally visible, shared and valued. In one example, Liz Lerman's *Hiking the Horizontal* (2011) discusses the wealth of experience she has gained throughout a career, and indeed, life, in dance. She describes a dance session in which mature dancers offer guidance and mentorship to younger dancers:

> Taking their turns, they danced more freely and more beautifully than I had ever seen in their university class. On the way back to campus they were full of excitement: 'I was never able to do triple turns before. What happened?' or 'My leg has never gone that high and with so much ease.' This happened so often I began to wonder why. I decided that they were dancing so well because they were so loved. The dance environment in which so many of

these students had grown up was harshly judgmental. It was a liberating experience for them to perform for an audience that offered such unreserved appreciation for their dancing and admiration for their bodies. (2011: 44)[5]

However, not all matured dancers seem to understand the importance of this. In 2013 when the *New York Times* journalist Joan Anderman asked the dance maker and dance artist Mark Morris the question 'How does a dancer know when it's time to stop?' his response was 'when you're nine months pregnant is one reason. And when you can't do the work you need to do'. Anderman went on to ask 'You don't dance much anymore', to which Morris replied 'I'm too old. I don't need to. And you get so tired of warming up' (Mark Morris [2013] NYTIMES. [ONLINE]).[6] Morris's position here offers debate regarding the importance of individuals being able to choose the journey they want,[7] as he places some value on being able to dance how one has always danced. My advocacy for the presence of ageing dance in performance rubs against traditional dance expectations and aims to create a space for ageing artists within performance, but I do not expect all ageing performers to want to continue to perform or engage in daily warm-up classes. I respect their decision.

By now, it is clear that I am not suggesting older dancers (or athletes) perform as they did when they were much younger dancing/performing bodies. In later life, there is a need for change and a somatic-ising or a re-languaging of the self in order to accommodate some form of the ageing process which would stop established artists (like Morris), who stated 'I'm too old', 'I don't need to', 'You get so tired of warming up'. The fact Morris says he gets tired of warming up is a possible indicator for the need to re-language his style. Morris's view is one which can evolve in terms of nostalgia and memory. By thinking he is too old signals the need to negotiate an embodiment of change as he needs to have a visibility and not shy away from the stage. His ageing presence would be a valuable marker for consciousness raising rather than being a 'body in waiting' for the next 'choreographic spark' or possibly feeling the need to stay in the wings while employing younger dancers to present work.

Despite these reflective comments from Morris in 2013, I had seen him perform a solo piece in 1995 as part of his company's UK tour at the Grand Theatre in Blackpool. It was a solo he had danced in his younger days and had revisited the work while nearing 40. It was the same year I saw Brown and although, as mentioned previously, I was younger (and traditional contemporary dance technique driven) I did appreciate his ability to own the stage through his subtle sense of humour and a performative element that, like Brown, had come into its own style. Although he was sweating profusely and (in parts) short of breath, this seemed to add to the richness of a body that was older and larger than the rest of his dance company members. He was presenting work that clearly had an embodiment spanning several years and executed this with what appeared to be an autonomy that came with his maturing age and wealth of performance experience. Morris was showing that dance can contain age and a larger frame and by doing so navigated away from the usual slender and youthful commodity body in dance performance.[8] Therefore, age becomes a characteristic through which an individual performing body offers diversity and richness: it should still therefore be embraced as part of the social and performing make up.

Moving away from stylised forms is one avenue by which dancers seek liberation from institutionalised technique. Liz Schwaiger suggests that ageing is a process: 'we are obviously not "young" one year and "old" the next, but fluid selves constantly in a process of becoming' (2012: 176). Schwaiger's earlier scholarship explores how postmodern dance is an example of how to combine new techniques and renegotiate one's dancing language (for my own experience of this in more detail, see Chap. 5 on *Falling Apart at the Seams*). According to Schwaiger, ageing artists no longer strive for technical accuracy and they recognise the dancer's body as an ordinary body. This results in a move away from codified, polished performance techniques and a movement which is more freeing (Schwaiger 2005: 112).

Lee (1989) notes how the decision to dance no longer has a profound effect on self-esteem. Lee discusses how dancing from an early age is embedded in one's ego identity, and the loss of the role of the dancer can thus be devastating: 'when a professional ballet dancer considers retirement, he/she is giving up a sense of self' (1989: 28—see also practitioner work on Jerôme Bel and Veronique Doisneau in Chap. 3). Lee attributes this to the youthful development stages of a dancer: 'an occupation identity begins to form during adolescent development, fusing self-identity with occupational identity' (Lee 1989: 27). For Lee, the development of a dancing identity is embedded within one's self-identity, and thus the decision to dance no longer requires a reconsideration of one's personal identity.[9] Therefore, my work considers ageing alongside identity, as the following section explores.

AGE AND IDENTITY

Within the literature reviewed so far, I have explored the challenges ageing presents to the mind and body, in which the dancing mind remains creatively capable, yet the process of ageing disrupts the body. I equally contested cultural expectations of ageing bodies in dance. In choosing to write about these experiences I have positioned the performer as self, writer and researcher/researched. This autobiographical process marks transitions in identity in relation to ageing, which are expressed through reflective writing and descriptions of bodily memories. Throughout, nostalgia provokes emotional responses, including the sense of loss, resistance and vulnerability. Sociologist, Steph Lawler observes how, 'identities are produced through the autobiographical work in which all of us engage every day' (2014: 26).

Identity has surfaced as widely theorised and applied in many areas of arts and sciences, resulting in Bauman's claim that 'identity is the loudest talk in town' (Bauman 2004: 7). In this context, there has been a subjective turn towards self-hood as a lens for academic studies. Identities are therefore constructed and reconstructed: individuals self-fashioning their own narratives in written forms. Lawler states:

> In narrating a story, social actors organise events into 'episodes' which make up the plot. In doing so, of course, they draw on memories. But, not only do they interpret those memories, the memories themselves are interpretations. It is not simply that memory is unreliable (although it is): the point is that memories are themselves social products. (Lawler 2014: 30)

Engaging with identity as a concept must come with a warning. The narratives related to identity which are produced should not be treated as static, rigid products. They serve to mark the fluidity and changeability of life stories and identities, and therefore are not the final word on a story. For Lawler, identity is not inflexible or unyielding, but unstable and variable. This leads to notions of identity as unreliable yet this is exactly what serves as a tool in terms of discussing dance and identity. The notion of identity as unfixed and radically changing leads us to appreciate multiplicities of possibilities. Catherine Bateson agrees:

> we need ways to tell stories that are interwoven and recursive, that escape from the linearity of print to incite new metaphors. I believe that the choices we face today are so complex that they must be rehearsed and woven together in narrative. (Bateson 2000: 247)

Therefore, dance and identity can serve as a tool for explorations of self-hood, including engaging with somatic practices. From this awareness of self, as indulgent, heuristic and self-serving as it may be critiqued, one develops an ethics of attention and care towards others' narratives. It could be argued that artists should never separate self from art, and Mooney's observation from the 1950s still rings true today: 'research is a personal venture which, quite aside from its social benefits, is worth doing for its direct contribution to one's own self-realization' (1957: 155). The casualty of self has been a result of researchers who strive for sanitised and idealised processes and outcomes from research.

While advocating identity as an important research tool, where the researchers' narratives are explored as part of the artistic process, I remain fully cognisant that there is no real access to the past. In terms of viewing the past, there is no neutral lens, as present-day life offers multiple inter-pretations. We reconstruct and read the narrative from the beginning with knowledge of the end. Lawler observes narrative as such a phenomenon: 'neither researcher nor researched can fully access or inhabit a past which is inevitably gone' (2002: 248). Paul Ricoeur (1991a) calls this 'narrative identity'. Yet this lack of direct objective route to exploring narrative should not mean it is a futile endeavour. It is certainly the present con-struction of the narrative which is important. The position of the present in relation to the past is what bears fruit, as Ricoeur states: '...narrative mediation underlines this remarkable characteristic of self-knowledge – that it is self-interpretation' (1991b: 198).

In working with the chaotic and disordered nature of biography and memory, it is clear that there is no direct access to an objective past. The notion of memory is clouded. Thomas Butler describes this failing as inherent to human nature: 'Did God do an imperfect job? [....] Or, is Forgetting i.e. the nonretrieval of most of the information that is pro-cessed in a lifetime, somehow part of the plan?' (1989: 15). Indeed, social scientists regard the importance of a present reinterpretation of past events as significant as the memory which is reconstructed. In this context, Elder comments that a selective reinterpretation of past events helps individuals make sense of their lives: 'memories of the past shape experience in the present, and the past may be reconstructed to fit the present' (1981: 110). So, the focus is not just on the life event being recalled, but on the process of selection by the recaller, as whether to include it as relevant to their past. Martin Kohli discusses this problematic nature of reconstruction, as he notes, 'there is at least some truth in what is being narrated ... there is some specifiable relation between the narrative reconstruction and the events to which it refers' (1981: 69). Steph Lawler agrees that

> there is no unmediated access to the 'facts of the matter', or to a straightforward and unmediated 'experience'. As the past is remembered, it is interpreted and reinterpreted in the light of the person's knowledge and understanding. (2014: 31)

Therefore, the memories which fuel my practice-led investigations are recalled and reshaped because of my own current thoughts and attitudes, and perhaps subconscious selection of what I recall, through a present lens, as significant or relevant. This is of specific importance as my dialogue with my past is reshaped, refocused and re/told in light of my research into current attitudes of an ageing self who dances, through the autoethnographic search and an autobiographical reflection into my life as a living archive.

Conclusion

Coupland's article 'Dance, Ageing and the Mirror' (2013) is concerned with issues of spectatorship and watchability: 'Dance makes bodies watchable, while ageing has been claimed to make bodies "unwatchable"' (2013: 3). One's self-identity can be paralysed when one cannot accept the process of ageing; a process in which one's body, mind and self-identity will continue to evolve. For Coupland, 'unwatchability' functions as an insult on the physical body and one's identity: 'unwatchability functions as an essentializing discourse, reducing the apparent essence of a personal identity to a physical self-assumed to be "spoiled" by age-marking, and consequently stigmatized' (2013: 6). Ageing is a process of becoming, according to Gullette:

> Your story must be a *becoming* ... one must recognize that one's dissatisfaction with one's appearance stems from the poisonous ageist propaganda one has internalized, and one must reconnect with one's distinctive life story and unique subjectivity. (1999: 55)

Connecting with one's life story and subjectivity is the platform for Chap. 3, where I move on to explore a practitioner review of practitioners who engage the theme of ageing within their dance making.

Notes

1. Similarly, GOLDS (Growing Old Disgracefully) in Canberra, Australia is aimed at over 55 movers, with a focus on fitness, mobility, sociability and creativity. See http://canberradancetheatre.org/classes/class-details.html
2. It must be acknowledged that the scholarship and practice informing this study is western in origin. For an interesting discussion on ageing in dance in Japanese culture, see Nakajima, N. (2011). The situation of dance in Japan is one we can learn from, where 'the presence of professional old dancers, such as Butoh artist Kazuo Ohno, challenges the Euro-American structures that relegate young professionals to contemporary dance and older amateurs to Community Dance' (2011: 100).
3. In 2014, Channel 4 produced a documentary which followed the lives on plus-sized individuals who learnt ballet technique in order to create a live performance. The programme, entitled *Big Ballet* sought to rebuff the idea that overweight dancers in performance would not catch on. As the theatre packed out for the final performance, filled with family and friends, it became clear this was a one-off performance experiment and ballet for larger dancers was still not mainstream or 'proper' ballet.
4. Dance scholar Linda Ashley has coined the term 'youthanasia' to describe dance as a youth-driven art form where the mature mover is not present. See http://germainewrites.com/2013/04/dance-and-aging/. [Accessed 29 August 2015.]
5. Within her prologue to the book, Lerman shares how she is interested 'in keeping professional dancers alive as human beings; in what dancers have to learn from people who have been in motion for over sixty years; in how much dancers know and how little we share it with the rest of the world; in how much dancers know and how little the rest of the world knows we know it; in the moment when people who are too fat, too clumsy, too old, too sick to dance actually step out and dance' (2011: x).
6. Available at: http://mobile.nytimes.com/2013/06/04/booming/mark-morris-on-dance-aging-and-immortality.html?pagewanted=all. [Accessed 11 April 2016.]
7. I detect a note of flippancy in Morris's comments, however. His own New York based company has been involved in a major project in terms of work with Parkinson's (http://danceforparkinsons.org [Accessed 29 August 2015]).
8. Within an interview with *New York Times Magazine* (9 July 1995). Mark Morris is asked 'what qualities are most important in a choreographer?' He replies 'Imagination and knowing when to stop. Just because you think it's interesting doesn't mean it actually is interesting' (http://www.nytimes.com/1995/07/09/magazine/sunday-july-9-1995-questions-for-mark-morris.html [Accessed 27 August 2015]).
9. For a discussion on ageing in dance in relation to self-esteem, see McMullin and Cairney (2004) and Lovatt (2011).

Bibliography

Amans, D. (2013) *Age and Dancing*. London: Palgrave.

Bateson, C. (2000) *Full Circle Overlapping Lives*. New York: Ballantine Books.

Bauman, Z. (2004) *Identity Conversations with Benedetto Vecchi*. Cambridge: Polity Press.

Butler, T. (1989) Memory, History, Culture and the Mind. Oxford: Blackwell.

Conway, S. and Hockey, J. (1998) 'Resisting the "Mask" of Old Age? The Social Meaning of Lay Health Beliefs in Later Life' *Ageing and Society*, 18(4). pp. 469–497.

Coupland, J. (2013) 'Dance, Ageing and the Mirror: Negotiating Watchability' in *Discourse and Communication*, 7(1). pp. 3–27.

Coupland, J. and Gwyn, R. (2003) *Discourse, the Body and Identity*. London: Palgrave.

Edward, M. and Newall, H. (2013) *Not With My Body Ya Don't! Ageing Dancers and the Habitus Turn*. Conference Paper, TaPRA, Unpublished.

Elder, G. H. (1981) 'History and the Life Course' in Betraux, D. (Ed.) Biography and Society: The Life History Approach in the Social Sciences. California: Sage. pp. 77—115.

Featherstone, M., Hepworth, M. and Turner, B. (1991) *The Body: Social Processes and Cultural Theory*. London: Sage.

Featherstone, M. and Wernick, A. (Eds.) (1995) *Images of Aging: Cultural Representations of Later Life*. London: Routledge.

Gullette, M. M. (1999) 'The Other End of the Fashion Cycle' in Woodward, K. (Ed.) Figuring Age: Women, Bodies, Generations. Bloomington: Indiana University Press, pp. 34–57.

Hepworth, M. (2003). 'Ageing Bodies: Aged by Culture' in Coupland, J. & Gwyn, R. (Eds.) *Discourse, the Body, and Identity*. New York: Palgrave Macmillan. pp. 80–107.

Kohli, M (1981) 'Account, Text, Method' in Bertaux, D. (ed.) *The Life History Approach in the Social Sciences*. California: Sage.

Lawler, S. (2014) *Identity*. Cambridge: Polity Press.

Lawler, S. (2002) 'Narrative in Social Research' in May, T. (Ed.) *Qualitative Research in Action*. London: Sage. pp. 242–58.

Lee, S. A. (1989). 'Retirement of a Professional Dancer' in *Dance Selected Current Research*, (1). pp. 63–77.

Lerman, L. (2011) *Hiking the Horizontal*. Middletown, CT: Wesleyan University Press.

Lovatt, P. (2011) 'Dance Confidence, Age and Gender' *Personality and Individual Differences*, 50(5). pp. 668-672.

McMullin J.A. and Cairney J. (2004) 'Self-Esteem and the Intersection of Age, Class, and Gender' *Journal of Aging Studies*, 18(1). pp. 75–90.

Mooney, R. L. (1957) 'The Researcher Himself' in *Research for Curriculum Improvement, Association for Supervision and Curriculum Development, 1957*

Yearbook. Washington, DC: Association for Supervision and Curriculum Development. pp. 154–187.

Morris, M. (2013 interview) http://www.nytimes.com/2013/06/04/booming/mark-morris-on-dance-aging-and-immortality.html

Nakajima, N. (2011) 'De-aging Dancerism? The Aging Body in Contemporary and Community Dance' *Performance Research*, 16(3). pp. 100–104.

Phoenix, C. and Sparkes, A. (2008) 'Athletic Body and Ageing in Context: The Narrative Construction of Experienced and Anticipates Selves in Time' in *Journal of Aging Studies*, 22(3). pp. 211–227.

Ricœur, P. (1991a) 'Life in Quest of Narrative' (trans. D. Wood) in Wood, D. (Ed.) *On Paul Ricœur: Narrative and Interpretation*. London: Routledge.

Ricœur, P. (1991b) 'Narrative Identity' (trans. D. Wood) in Wood, D. (Ed.) *On Paul Ricœur: Narrative and Interpretation*. London: Routledge.

Schwaiger, E. (2012) *Ageing, Gender, Embodiment and Dance*. Hampshire: Palgrave Macmillan.

Schwaiger, E. (2009) 'Performing Youth: Ageing, Ambiguity and Bodily Integrity' in *Social Identities*, 15(2). pp. 273–287.

Schwaiger, E. (2005) 'Performing One's Age: Cultural Constructions of Aging and Embodiment in Western Theatrical Dancers' in *Dance Research Journal*, 37(1). pp. 107–120.

Sparkes, A. (2009) 'Ethnography and the Senses: Challenges and Possibilities' in *Qualitative Research in Sport and Exercise*, 1(1). pp. 21–37.

Thomas, H. (2013) *The Body and Everyday Life*. New York: Routledge.

CHAPTER 3

Mature Movers

Abstract In focusing on the rare examples of ageing in performance, I provide an overview of practice work within the fields of ageing and performance. To contextualise the discussion of the visibility of mature movers, I discuss the complexities of sourcing practice-based evidence, as the process of performance documentation is often varied and inconsistent. Such subjective processing means that a 'one design fits all' approach cannot be adopted. In providing examples of mature movers, I look at two particular areas: firstly, mature movers who do not necessarily explore the theme of ageing in their work; and secondly performers who actively address the theme of ageing who are actually ageing, using their own experience as a source for creating performance. Attention is also given to performance-based works which address the theme of ageing from a non-ageing perspective, exploring the inevitable debility of the performing body from a youthful lens.

Keywords Mature • Documentation • Life stories • Manifesto • Aged • Life narratives

This chapter provides an overview of practice-based work within the fields of ageing and performance. The first section explores the complexities of locating practice-based sources, as the process of performance documentation is often varied and inconsistent. It is a complex process as the

M. Edward, *Mesearch and the Performing Body*,
https://doi.org/10.1007/978-3-319-69998-1_3

research is particular to the creator and therefore a 'one design fits all' approach cannot be adopted. Following an examination of varied attempts to archive 'bodily change' in ageing performers, the discussion then addresses practitioners from two emerging areas: firstly, mature performers, who do not necessarily explore the theme of ageing in their work; and secondly, performers who actively address the theme of ageing who are actually ageing, using their own experience as a source for creating performance. Attention is also given to performance-based works which address the theme of ageing from a non-ageing perspective, exploring the inevitable debility of the performing body from a youthful lens. My own work spans all three categories, and references to works detailed come from my own reflections. The chapter concludes with a consideration of the gaps within current discourse on ageing in performance which needs to be addressed in terms of extending the debate about longevity in performance.

Documenting Performance

> Performance's only life is in the present. Performance cannot be saved, recorded, documented, or otherwise participate in the circulation of representations *of* representations: once it does so, it becomes something other than performance. (Phelan 1993: 146)

Phelan's view points to a temporality of performance which, once documented, becomes something else other than performance. Auslander labels such documentation as 'performative of performance' (2006: 5). It enters a new skin. Documentation within performing arts, and academia more generally, is a term which is often wrongly synonymised with 'evidence'. In my attempt to develop Phelan's position, I refer to Piccini and Rye who provide a new approach to the thorny issue of documentation in performance, by recognising the alternative product which is an outcome of the process of documentation. They call this 'telling otherwise' and acknowledge that any reconstruction of the practice, in documented form, renders the practice elusive: 'there is no such thing as documentation, per se' (2009: 46). Following the philosophical footsteps of Paul Ricoeur (1991), 'telling otherwise' is a method of documentation which is aware of the false position of 'evidence' within archived documentation, but seeks to keep alive a sense of the performance within an ongoing discussion of 'what might be' (Piccini and Rye 2009: 46). There is no real access to the past and no fixed identity of the performance once it is over, indeed, it often becomes something 'other' afterwards, for example, a video, a photograph.

The issue of documentation and securing material evidence of the performance is further compounded through consideration of the complexities of performance knowledge. Within his work on acting and the theatre, Watson notes how performance knowledge is 'ephemeral', 'idiosyncratic' and 'amorphous' (2009: 89). Accordingly, for Watson, performance knowledge 'can be talked about, even committed to paper, but it only exists in the doing' (2009: 89); it becomes an embodied knowledge which is stored in a liminal space of the performing body, which cannot be successful in disseminating a full understanding and appreciation of its knowledge, complexities and experience. For Watson, access to performance knowledge through the word, either spoken or written, is restrictive in its transmission. Crystalline forms may function as part of a narrative relating to the performance, but they are always different to the work itself.

I appreciate the dichotomy in utilising the written work to access an archive of practice-based works. Engaging with practice-based performance work should not simply be a written undertaking, and the accompanying photographs in this book form part of a migration into a new space where the practice work has been documented in different skins and different formats. The written word and the photographic work all provide different means of accessing aspects of the performance which itself is a non-stable historical event. These new sources combined negotiate its migration from a historical occurrence to a legacy in the present. Any discussion of practice from this point no longer views it as a perfect past event, but one which has an ongoing, evolving and living memory, which is its continuous legacy. This is not to say that the performance event is prioritised or privileged over the legacy material; they are all part of the same practice and they keep alive the performance, thus becoming mutually dependable in terms of documentation, sustainability and relevance. Within the following section, attention now turns to the legacies of practice-based work within the field of age(ing) and performance.

PRACTICE LEGACIES

Fergus Early and Jacky Lansley's (2011) exploration into the personal voices and experiences of twelve mature dance practitioners is a relevant starting point to investigate the subjective and varied languages across their participants and their relationship with dance as a cultural form. Their collection of interviews collated in the edited volume *The Wise Body* offers positive dialogue from older dancers yet this text could be seen as 'unwise', as the stigma relating to older movement of flesh and bones still prevails in some cultural circles, with age discrimination in dance being the constant threat to youthful maturation. Similarly, Diane Amans' *Age and Dancing* (2013) provides an overview of older movers and community dance practice. More relevant to my practice is not a review of existent literature on older dance practitioners or practice, but consideration of performance legacies which have been used to denote the performance polemic of age and dance. As noted previously, the practices I explore fall into the following areas:

1) Examples of mature performers, who do not necessarily use the theme of ageing as their work.
2) Performers who actively address the topic of ageing within the content of their work and are ageing.
3) Performers who actively address the theme of ageing within the context of their work but are not aged—potential exploration of the fear of ageing.

Therefore, for readability I have mobilised these three categories into headings below for ease of discussion: mature movers, the theme of ageing and aged before time. The practitioners and practices I explore below are based on my own spectatorship at the live performances of these works. All works were viewed and experienced by myself in the UK. In relating my spectator experiences through the written form, I note my detailing of the performance is 'telling otherwise', and provides a mere blink of an eye snapshot of the essence of each performance.

MATURE MOVERS

Generación del Ayer (Yesterday's Generation 1996–) is a Chilean-based dance company whose aim is to break the established cycle of dancers' careers ending when they reach maturity. Their philosophy is that older artists still have much to say on stage. Consisting of senior citizens, the members engage in creating dance theatre for themselves and by themselves. The choreographic practices do not necessarily cover themes of ageing. In 2014, I was fortunate enough to meet with the group and see their work *lo que me dio el agua* (what water gave me), in which subtle gentle movements animated the piece, based on the work of the Mexican artist, Freda Kahlo.

Within the UK, the Company of Elders (1989–) is an over-60s company consisting of 28 performers, who may have attained their bus passes, but still have the creative capacity to perform. The company has garnered much interest from a range of renowned choreographers and in 2007, their dance work *In Your Rooms* premiered, an adaptation of Hofesh Shechter's original choreography to suit the bodies and life histories of the older dancers.[1]

Another such example of existing work being adapted to mature forms is Pina Bausch's *Kontakthof.* The work, originally choreographed and performed in 1978 depicted the same choreography executed by both younger and older bodies. Bausch depicts how older bodies no longer have to become backstage coaches for younger flesh. She is age-innovative in allowing mature movers the visible presence to explore their own physical capacity in a culture that is prone to discriminate.

Mats Ek and his partner Ana Laguna continue to create and perform distinctive works, such as *Memory* (2004) and *Potato* (2006). *Memory* explores how memory is an embodied form, rather than a recall of a factual event, While *Potato* acknowledges dance as a basic, yet nutritious art.

A further mature dance artist who has successfully negotiated age(ing) and been able to preserve a dance biography and codified embodied dance technique is the classical ballet dancer Alessandra Ferri. Ferri's return to dance and performing after a long career break to spend time with her family is demonstration that the body's dancing biography and physical capital does not have to be severely ruptured, cast aside or lack physical power after an absence from performing. When Ferri dances, we can clearly see she has maintained the ability to execute such highly technical dance forms. Dancing in Wayne McGregor's ballet *Woolf Works* (2015), which is based on the author Virginia Wolf, the viewer can see how Ferri's human entity gives rise to her dancing practice and is able to meet the rigorous demands of classical dance techniques. Ferri's dancing, as with others mentioned in this book, requires the spectator to take notice of the older performing presence and illuminates the ageing body's resistance to the 'decline' of a dancing career. More recently Ferri has been the 'face' of the beauty cosmetic No.7²; the TV commercial projects her as a much younger 19-year-old dancing which is then juxtaposed alongside her current older self. The two dancers engage side by side on screen, where the matured Ferri demonstrates that she can still execute the same dance form as she did over 30 years ago.

The Theme of Age

Generación del Ayer, noted previously, have also produced work which incorporates the theme of ageing. Within their UK tour under the sponsorship of the Foreign Affairs Secretary of Chile (2014), they performed various works. *Thresholds* was physically more impactive than *Lo que me dio el agua*, which highlighted their control over exercising their contemporary techniques. I remained mesmerised by their physical core strength, and the passion and dedicated approach to performance was palpable. The choreographic note under the title advertising the piece states: 'Beings that are in search of the dance they lost, or believed lost, because their body said NO. For all they had been, they will dance and keep on dancing until the last betrayal of their being.'³

In *That Paper Boy: un solo pour Dominique Mercy* (2014), age is literally highlighted through a fluorescent light which shines along the contours of Dominque Mercy's 64-year-old body. Mercy was born in 1950, and has been a member of Bausch's Tanztheater Wuppertal since 1977. In the 2014 piece, both he and Pascal Merighi, a younger Wuppertal colleague, duet. Both dance the same material to the lyrics 'when I am older'. There is a vast age gap between them both, yet there is no distinction between ability and performance presence. There is a performance wisdom worthy of note here, in which time and experience have both enabled Mercy to explore, understand and share his craft. Mercy was one of Bausch's original members of the company and Merighi joined much later. Mercy and Merighi's abilities were incomparable in terms of executing the contemporary dance, with fast-paced bursts of energetic choreography. I preferred watching Mercy. He drew me in, and not because of his age I would like to think, but because of his performing presence and technical ability. Both performed with toned bodies, executing their technical ability without any inconsistencies, thereby demonstrating that decades of embodied performance knowledge trump youth. Equally of French origin is the work of Jerôme Bel, invited to choreograph a ballet for the

Opéra Paris. Bel sought to present a documentary of the work of Véronique Doisneau. Doisneau, on stage, discusses how she is at retirement age, and views her career retrospectively while commenting on the career-span of a ballerina. Bel used this solo performance as a revelation of life; he states:

> I chose a solo format because I wanted to 'contrast' Véronique Doisneau to the Corps de Ballet as a company and an institution. I wanted to hear what she herself thought about the Opéra, her career and dancing. Her view is very subjective, but I feel this singularity is important. That's why I gave the piece her name, *Véronique Doisneau,* so that there was no misunderstanding. (Jerôme Bel [2004] jeromebel.fr [ONLINE])[4]

Solo work spotlights the individual subjectivity, whereas ensemble work in ballet is often intermittent and elides identity.

Another example of solo work is Liz Aggiss, who performed *The English Channel* (2015). Exploring her own youth from childhood and narrating her biographical experiences, from singing about the imposition of table manners from her parents to narrating her desire to become a punk. She discusses partying as a mature woman, where one gin gets her tipsy. Aggiss engages in German Expressionist dance forms, and performs a series of monologues which juxtaposes humour alongside the theme of ageing. Aggiss's work included both a parody and homage to German Expressionism. Similarly, her work *Slap and Tickle* (2016) also addresses themes of ageing for the female body and again Aggiss puts on display her age-autobiography. Within *Slap and Tickle* Aggiss asks the audience 'are there any leaky mothers in the house?' while delivering a range of physically absurd comedic moments.

Wendy Houston is another practitioner who describes how hitting 50 'introduced the concept of history into my life' (2011: 33). She discusses how being an older dancer denotes a discrepancy between the feel of movement and the look of movement:

> Maybe this accounts for the tendency of older dancers and movers to look as if they are lost in their own nostalgic dancing past. Looking like deluded idiots unwilling to surrender their prime – and unable to enter the present. The body has imprints of moves running around it that reside in another era. (2011: 37)

Houston performed a solo *Haunted, Daunted and Flaunted* in the 1990s. Within the piece, she uses comedy to alleviate serious social critique which challenges misconceptions about movement. Such critiques are also levied at self, as Houston questions herself:

> I find myself asking people if I look embarrassing when I move. If I look like I think I'm younger than I am. I did see a review saying I was doing the moves of someone half my age, but I couldn't tell if that meant I should stop doing them or carry on. (2011: 37)

I watched Houston perform her solo at the Green Room in Manchester, UK. She captivated me through her strong and dynamic femininity and ability to deliver the spoken word while delivering a range of fast-paced frenetic movements. So, in response to her above citation, 'carry on!' I say!

Wim Vandekeybus re/presented his first choreography *What the Body Does Not Remember* at The Lowry in Salford, UK. In this 2015 performance, he danced the same choreography that was first shown in 1987. Vandekeybus's own choreographic journey into his living embodied dancing archive of flesh and bones was one that maintained the same level of energy and athleticism as the youthful performance from the Ultima Vez company, with which he collaborated. Within the publicity for the performance, Vandekeybus comments:

> When I watch the performance, I can feel the original passion and energy all over again. At the time I was utterly sick of all that aesthetic stuff, that 'pretending'. I wanted raw emotion, physical power and guts. Now, decades later, we are still throwing stones in the revival of *What the Body Does Not Remember*. To me that proves not only that a lot is possible, but also that what is possible can also last. (Wim Vandekeybus [2015] ultimavez.com. [ONLINE])[5]

Several community-based dance projects have also paved a positivist pathway for the third age on the stage. In 1980, Liz Lerman, working for Dance Exchange, established *Dancers of the Third Age*, a group of senior citizen dancers; and Third Stage Dance company promoting a return to dance for professionals who have long hung up their ballet slippers or dusted off their bare feet. Third Stage acknowledges that dance is in the blood, and this should be honoured in spite of one's life experiences or abilities.

AGED BEFORE TIME

After having considered mature movers and performance practices which explore the theme of ageing, attention now turns to a subjective view of my own practice as an ageing performer. It is very rare that contemporary dance practices explore the theme of ageing with youthful performers, and my creation and performance of *Falling Apart at the Seams* (2008) was to demarcate the crossroads of my self-realisation as a dancer beginning to age. To discuss a performance about ageing dance when the choreographer and performer is in his mid-30s seems a sharp contrast to the third age dance performers and practices detailed earlier. Yet, to me at the time, I was beginning to become aware of my own negotiations in performance. Further details about the piece is discussed in Chap 5, but for now, I note how the performance explores the theme of ageing and presents the decline and decay of the dancer, of which I was fearful. As part of this research process, I am now in a position where I can comfortably claim no longer to be fearful, but there is always the presence of a melancholic memory when ageing dancers re-create and perform.

Within the piece, I collaborated with dance artist Julia Griffin and octogenarian June Sands,[6] a British Variety veteran who danced and sang with me in *Falling Apart at the Seams* (2008). June reperformed her Variety favourites, while in separate sections, Julia and I explored the limitations of ageing performers in terms of physicality and declining ability, but with a passion for dance which could not be extinguished (further reflections on the rehearsal process is found in Chap. 5).

CONCLUSION: AN AGE MANIFESTO

It is important to note that the practitioners described in this chapter as mature entered the profession at an age of experimentation. In their youth, they were pioneers of dance practice, and they should not leave the art form quietly during the night.[7] Dance continues to change with them, and it is through their practice as they mature that ageing dancers are being appreciated. The examples of work produced and performed by mature movers demonstrate how renowned older artists continue to create and perform powerful work, through bodies which hold rich embodied techniques, forms and dance experience.[8] Their contribution to the age debate in dance is visible; and it is this visibility which acts as a catalyst for spectatorship, discussion, research and empowerment. Conferences relating to dance and age in the UK can be dated back to 1997, of which one was named Beyond the Tea Dance. However, it is over the past ten years we see an increase in interest and scholarship, with a rise in the number of conferences: What's Age Got To Do With It? (2007),[9] Ageing Artfully Conference (2011),[10] Age Watch: Dance and Life Long Well Being (2013),[11] Art of Age Conference (2014).[12]

Yet despite the burgeoning interest in dance and ageing, any discussion of older artists often uses present continuous verbs forms, such as 'continues to dance' alongside adverbs such as 'still' and 'again'. I too am guilty of this at times, yet therein lies the rub. The assumption still prevails that the rare performance of mature movers is often nostalgic or seeks to recreate previous work. The language used in reviews to describe their work is almost apologetic or explanatory in seeking to justify the presence of mature movers on the stage. As a society, we have set in stone legislation which ensures inclusion and equality of rights to protected characteristics such as race, disability, gender and sexuality. Yet, within dance we still see companies who are fully inclusive but seek to explain the ability of their performers. We need to move away from these explanatory paradigms and label dance as dance, without further explanation of its performers or its agenda and only then will assimilation for such 'subgroups' be realistic.

The case study examples of my performance work, detailed in Chap. 5 onwards, are examples where my own negotiation of age and identity are being worked out. Each practice-led piece has been created and performed at different junctures of my process of 'becoming'. *Falling Apart at the Seams* (2008) explores fears of ageing in performance at a time when I still considered my technique as solid and my age as youthful. *Council House Movie Star* (2012) explores different embodiments, social, gendered, physical, as I revisited my working-class roots, my early days of performing drag and how I had gained weight and was negotiating a new body size. *Dying Swans and Dragged Up Dames* (2013, 2014) revisits past embodied techniques and how my body executes such movements as I am now mature and heavier. For now, attention turns to the subjective methodology I employ as my research tool, detailed in the following chapter, on methodologies.

NOTES

1. Reasons for why mature professional dancers would return to perform in such works are merely speculative. Aside from possible remunerations, there could also be a desire to explore what the body remembers.
2. This advert (for face cream) could also be reinforcing negativities towards age(ing) by advocating a need for 'anti-age(ing)' facial products.

3. Programme for *Elixir Festival*, Sadler's Wells, September 2014.
4. Jerome Bel. 2004. JeromeBel. [ONLINE] Available at: http://www.jeromebel.fr/textsandinterviews/detail?textInter=veronique%20doisneau%20%20paris%20national%20opera. [Accessed 11 April 2016].
5. Available at: http://www.ultimavez.com/en/productions/what-body-does-not-remember. [Accessed 11 April 2016].
6. Further reading on my process with June can be read in Edward, M. and Newall, H. (2012) 'Temporality of the Performing Body: Tears, Fears and Ageing Dears'. *Management, Expression, Interpretation* Edited by: Andrze, j Dańcza, k. ID Press.http://www.inter-disciplinary.net/probing-the-boundaries/making-sense-of/pain/project-archives/2n/.
7. Holt et al. note 'By the mid-1970s, when dance as a discipline entered higher education in the UK, the impact of American postmodern dance and British New Dance had been developing for a decade or more. This combined new trend in dance began to have a significant influence on many practitioners across the UK, as a source of innovation. Many of these practitioners were appointed to work as dance "animateurs" or community dance artists in arts venues and community settings as the driving force in the significant development of community dance programmes across the UK'. http://ausdance.org.au/articles/details/dance-in-higher-education-in-the-uk. [Accessed 19 February 2016.]
8. In one personal example of this, in 1998 I was awarded a bursary from Liverpool's Merseyside Dance Initiative to attend a residency in dance improvisation. Here I met (and shared dance experiences) with Mary Prestidge a former Ballet Rambert dancer, British Olympic gold medallist winner and one of the X6 British new dance pioneers. Mary was much older than I was and she danced with a real sense of autonomy coupled with a physical and conceptual intelligence.
9. http://www.danceuk.org/news/article/whats-age-got-do-it/. [Accessed 29 August 2015.]
10. http://www.communitydance.org.uk/DB/publications/ageing-artfully-the-baring-foundation.html. [Accessed 29 August 2015.]
11. http://www.agewatch.org.uk/fitness/dance-and-lifelong-well-being/. [Accessed 29 August 2015.]
12. http://www.sadlerswells.com/whats-on/2014/Elixir-Festival-The-Art-of-Age-Conference/. [Accessed 29 August 2015.]

Bibliography

Amans, D. (2013) *Age and Dancing*. London: Palgrave.
Auslander, P. (2006) 'The Performativity of Performance Documentation' in *A Journal of Performance and Art*, 28 (3). pp. 1–10.

Early, F. and Lansley, J. (2011) *The Wise Body.* Chicago: Intellect, University of Chicago Press.

Houston, W. (2011) 'Some Body and No Body: The Body of a Performer' [sic] in Pitches, J. and Popat, S. (Eds.) *Performance Perspectives: A Critical Introduction.* New York: Palgrave Macmillan.

Phelan, P. (1993) *Unmarked: The Politics of Performance.* London: Routledge

Piccini, A. and Rye, C. (2009) 'Of Fevered Archives and the Quest for Total Documentation' in Allegue, L., Jones, S., Kershaw, B., and Piccini, A. (Eds.) *Practice-as-Research: In Performance and Screen.* New York: Palgrave Macmillan. pp. 34–49.

Ricœur, P. (1991) 'Life in Quest of Narrative' (trans. D. Wood) in Wood, D. (Ed.) *On Paul Ricœur: Narrative and Interpretation.* London: Routledge.

Watson, I. (2009) 'An Actor Prepares: Performance as Research (PAR) in the Theatre' in Riley, S. and Hunter, L. (Eds.) *Mapping Landscapes for Performance as Research.* New York: Palgrave Macmillan.

CHAPTER 4

Me/thodologies

Abstract In this chapter, I focus on how artists engage with reflective methodologies when creating performance. The focus is on methodologies in its plural form, recognising the postmodern assortment of academic thought processes that are all intertwined with self as researcher, artists and performer. I argue that methodologies relating to experience and subjective life events are inevitably less scientific leading to fluid outcomes. The process of creating performance is complex and multiple. Heuristic, autobiographical and autoethnographical research methodologies are individualist and subjective. I consider myself as the *researcher researched* or *researched researcher*, and I discuss the duality of both roles, encapsulating the notion of self as part of the research process: mesearch.

Keywords Methodologies • Researcher • Autoethnographical • Reflexivity • Mesearch • Heurism

This chapter utilises the term methodologies within its plural form, as mixed methodologies underpin my work. Therefore, the chapter contains a discussion of a postmodern assortment of academic thought processes that are all intertwined with 'me' as researcher, artist and performer. Methodologies relating to experience and subjective life events are inevitably less scientific, leading to fluid outcomes which are not fixed or measured in terms of data production. The methodologies I have employed have served to inform my work processes; they are complex and multiple. As I have researched and incorporated elements of others' methodologies, mine too will never be duplicable for others to mobilise in the entire format. Therefore, the various practices engaged here together are distinct, related to and emerging from my own particular research endeavour. This chapter begins with a discussion of the complexities of managing multiple methodologies, and my subsequent exploration of methodologies bears in mind one of my initial research questions: how do I, as a performer, engage with reflective methodologies when creating performance?

MIXING ME AND METHODS

The borderlands between heurism, autoethnography and autobiography are hazy. In this work I offer the following simplistic distinctions between my definitions. Heuristic inquiry is an imperfect methodology which serves as a starting point to begin exploring self as research, providing only a general or immediate starting point to my research. Autobiography deals with the content of one's lived experiences; while autoethnography is the detailed process by which one seeks to research and make sense of one's lived experiences in the hope of knowledge transfer, whether that is self-knowledge or knowledge for others. Within my practical work, autobiographical and autoethnographical processes aim to advance my self-understanding of ageing through performance cultures. This is an attempt to challenge, re-write and re-*right* the self from cultural and social assumptions, representations and recurrent discrimination surrounding age(ing) in performance. My work contributes to subjective research conducted on the subversion or querying of ageing in performance, especially in terms of a self-dialogue.

Subjective research moves away from longer-standing notions of what constitutes research and 'the historical mistrust of the self as a topic of research' (Dobie 2010: 181) by challenging the established expectations that researchers should have a neutral voice. The lived research I present, as an integral element to my work, is no less rigorous than that of a science-based inquiry 'but the empirical data may be different as they take the form of subjective experience, discernment and direct knowing' (Hiles 2002: 1). In addition to the performance practices as an outcome of my research, I can also celebrate the embodied lived knowledge gained through the emotional and physical marks of time that have become etched within me. It is the exploration of an already embodied process, projected through a thread of multi-faceted works and writings, which attempts to engage and challenge spectators through their own self-recognition, locale and experience(s).

A Process of Reflexivity

Heuristic, autobiographical and autoethnographical research as method-ologies are individualist and subjective. As scholar and performance maker Tami Spry notes: 'in autoethnographic methods, the researcher is the epis-temological and the ontological nexus upon which the process turns' (2001: 189). As a researcher, I have become increasingly interested in the exploration and documentation of self through a lived experience that can find a way into being articulated into a personalised framework of textual analyses or a 'bespoke research methodology' (Parker-Starbuck and Mock 2011: 210) and how my body 'might become or produce performance spaces' (Parker-Starbuck and Mock 2011: 210) through a shift in how I engage my flesh in variable contexts. In addition to providing a framework for myself-as-researched, my work also generates new knowledge for myself and about myself. This provides a deeper insight and authority to my practice that has ultimately been born out of ontology of the self. In adopting this method, I encourage other practitioners to form a relation-ship with themselves in terms of documenting and disseminating their work as they age. The micro-processes of social interactions between per-formance and society are essential underpinnings of my performance worlds.

Sociologist Carol Rambo Ronai provides an excellent example of sub-jective research that allows the researcher's position to be disclosed, nay embraced. In her text *On Loving and Hating my Mentally Retarded Mother* (1997), Rambo Ronai states:

> Sociological introspection makes the interior world, or subjectivity of the researcher in question, the object of study. Fantasies, dreams, emotions and accounts of lived experience, (subjects normally ignored or hidden in the world of research) are highlighted not only for abstract analysis, but also for the reader who is invited to evaluate the text based on an unusual criteria for the social sciences. (1997: 6)

(INTER)DISCIPLINING ME AND MESEARCH[1]

My research is heavily rooted in interdisciplinary practice which is both autobiographical and autoethnographical, as represented through my existing body of practice spanning nearly two decades. My writing and performances bring about a first person biographical perspective. This, in turn, represents a self-determination and an authority of my own practice. Autoethnography serves thus as a 'resource for authorizing oneself being and doing reflexivity in practice' (Skeggs 2002: 349). From this, I am interested in exploring what Kershaw and Nicholson term 'productive instabilities between existing epistemological practices and ontological results' (2011: 2). My practice work then uses the tool of my body which serves as an archive and source of history ripe for exploration. In this way, I am both the subject and object of my research. This is a dual role and one which is intuitively negotiated. Sullivan warns that by adopting such a position 'the process changes both perspectives because creative and critical inquiry is a reflexive process' (2010: 45). This relationship with oneself, one's mind and one's body is a complex one, as I construct an interwoven '...'ideological' relationship between the [self] archival researcher and stuff in the document boxes and storage cabinets...' (Kershaw and Nicholson 2011: 5) with which I term the amalgamation of my research methodologies as *mesearching*.

Acknowledging that my research methodology is grounded in autobiographical and autoethnographical principles, I offer an alternative definition and rationale for the term mesearch that might be a better lexicon rather than the term autoethnography. This is not a trendy new, poststructuralist coinage, but an attempt at finding the correct term to define my research practice. In simple terms, mesearch is the creative inquiry into self as a living archive.

First, mesearch is a less academic and more accessible term. This is particularly suited to disseminate work to non-academic audiences; I offer the term as particularly suited to the discipline of performing arts and communicating effectively with audience members (see Fig. 4.1). Indeed, there is an irony in being a practitioner engaging in academic writing which has its own expectations in terms of structure, rigidity and form. For me, academic writing sometimes restricted my self-expression just as much as ballet did during my formative dance training. I needed to discover alternative ways for self-expression, which was not possible for me through ballet and other rigid technical forms. The same applied to

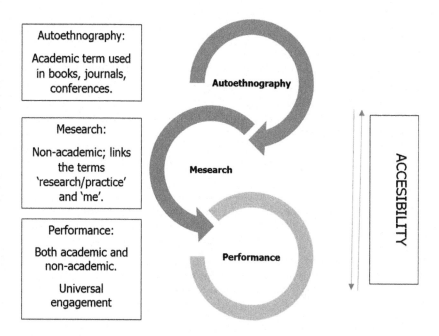

| Autoethnography: |
| Academic term used in books, journals, conferences. |

| Mesearch: |
| Non-academic; links the terms 'research/practice' and 'me'. |

| Performance: |
| Both academic and non-academic. |
| Universal engagement |

Fig. 4.1 Diagram to demonstrate the relationship between autoethnography, mesearch and performance

research undertaken within academia: the structures felt alien at times. Self-expression was lost, masked or hidden behind a smokescreen of expectations from the scholarly community. My languages—dance and writing—became identified and identifiable by their lack of fit, and mesearch enables them to express this periphery position. In one pertinent example, the need to find a more accessible term emerged during my practice-led work *Council House Movie Star* (see Chap. 6). The documenting of how the work was autoethnographic, via accompanying exegesis, was displayed throughout the gallery on information boards linked to the research aims and outcomes. In an anecdotal aside which provides impetus for the need of accessibility, I recall one particular afternoon while in drag during the performance when I overheard a spectator reading through one of the boards to her companion, who stated loudly 'What is this auto-whatsit on about? I don't understand any of this. Let's go see that drag queen again!' It was not until the public started to question the term that

I started to reflect on my possibly needing a simpler terminology for dissemination, as performance research should always be reachable to audiences in terms of impact and value.

Second, my rejection of the academic term autoethnography in favour of mesearch means that lengthy explanations of non-neutrality, or conversely, detailed descriptions to justify subjectivity, are no longer needed.[2] Arising from feminist sociological research, the absence of author is no longer a veil to academic writing. Miriam David (2003) provides a helpful analogy, in which she describes abstract positioning of the author as Oz without a screen and a speaker. Jolly sees autobiographical contributions as 'not to confess sins but to be seen as well as to see' (2005: 214). From the outset mesearch posits the word as clearly subjective.

My third rationale builds on the solid foundations which have been developed by pioneering autoethnographic researchers, which allows me to use mesearch as an approach to research. Within the term mesearch the personal first person pronoun encapsulates the individualised nature of the work, whereas autoethnography contains no personal pronoun. It is therefore a more appropriate semantic. It means the researcher does not seek to hide in grammar essentialism, where ethnographers and autoethnographers can still be grouped under the academically safe umbrella 'we'/'us'. It uses the personal voice and knows what this voice sounds like. Probyn's use of an autobiographical voice acknowledges the tension between this pronoun game, as she endeavours 'to construct ways of thinking that are marked by "me" but that do not efface actively or through omission the ways in which "she" may see differently' (1993: 4).

Finally, mesearch acknowledges the continuous nature of the search for self-hood, rather than relying on the assumption of self as a stable entity. An autoethnographical account is often written using past narratives, yet the interpretation and documentation of past events is a present action. Anna Fisk, in exploring feminist thought and its relation to literature notes how stories are not something we have already in us, which are in need of extraction, as the common autoethnographical position would have us believe:

> We do not look inside ourselves and find out stories there, submerged and waiting to be brought out into the light. The stories we tell about ourselves are produced—albeit from the 'stuff' of experience, however fragmented and unreliable our memory of it—within particular contexts and for particular purposes. (2014: 10)

Within *Council House Movie Star* (see Chap. 6), the set was populated with actual objects from my childhood: ornaments from my parents' and grandparents' house, personal memorabilia from my 1970s and 1980s council house upbringing were actually precious objects and memories to me, and there they were, all laid out for all to revel over, evoking different memories for other people who shared a common static object. The memory signifiers were laid out there for people to touch, tarnish and, sadly, damage and steal.

Autobiographical Inquiry: Be(yond) Myself

In later years, I realised that a biographical paradigm or explorative/transformative work about me and the experiences I have encountered could be communicated on a broader level. This involved the use of multi-disciplines, recontextualising themes and narratives, enhancing understandings through the interpretive and experiential paradigms. My previous self-indulgent attitude towards biography in performance began to change. Biographical performance can be an agent for personal exploration, individually and among audience members. Presenting lived experience to an audience in immersive ways is similar to talking to one another. You 'speak' about the personal in crafted (and sometimes less scripted) ways hoping to engage people on their many levels. In his book, *Dangerous Border Crossers* (2000), Gomez explores the subjective self in art. He argues, 'I only write or make art about myself when I am completely sure that the biographical paradigm intersects with larger social and cultural issues' (Gomez 2000: 7). As my work shared borders with cross-sectional social, cultural and political themes, such as ageing, sexuality, gender, poverty, I too intersect with wider thematic issues of relevance.

The physical and emotional challenges life presents me as I age, such as a diminishing dancing presence, physical disruptions, relational departures of dying relatives and friendships now foreign to me, can be journeyed and interrogated through a reflexivity and a writing of my work. Here, I can celebrate the lived knowledge gained through the emotional and physical marks of time that have become etched within me. Highlighting the fruitfulness of autobiography, Campbell and Harbord state:

> Autobiography is of interest precisely for the disruptions that it throws up as well as for the connections that can be made across different generic and disciplinary boundaries without necessarily performing dissolution of borders. (2002: 2)

Deirdre Heddon's work on autobiography and performance is significant in representing dance from experience. Heddon states 'the challenge
that continues to face practitioners is that of navigating a path between
dislodging dominant cultural representations by showing other representations drawn from experience' (2006: 31). The examples discussed in
Chap. 3—for example, Brown and Morris's ability to dance in their older
years—serve to move current organised notions of dancing as a youthful
phenomenon. Dance needs older visible dancing bodies which can dis-
lodge and move ageing and ability discrimination. As with all activism,
visibility of ageing is needed for it to become normalised within the performance arena. The continuous presence of age within performance
would break down expectations of youthful performers. Simply, it is
imperative that there is a visibility through further representation of ageing performers, which would serve to remove ageing dancers from their
abject status. What is required for ageing dancers is the process of a continuous and permeating presence and visibility. The projection of ageing
bodies challenges normative assumptions of youth which have dominated
performance visibility. Incorporating the markers of ageing and the heuris-
tics of physical ageing into dance performance has rich potential. This
certainly enriches range and dexterity. I hope to expand the cultural and
social significance of the ageing performer, through developing a deeper
understanding of performing my own age and a body reflexive practice,
where 'interpretations of and responses to the body are situated in social
relations, in interactions and in the context of institutions that serve to
construct and reconstruct those relations and institutions' (Laz 1998:
508).

As the body comes with objectification, in relation to gender, sexual
characteristics, ethnicity and so on, Leder notes how this takes on the
characteristics of one having a 'meat presence' (1990). Bodies described as
'meat' or a 'meat presence' implies a non-valued, almost consumerist status. Thomas attentively reminds us that such a position is temporal, and it
is this 'meat presence' that 'should not be viewed as a fixed entity' (Thomas
2013: 15). As a temporal status, the construction and reconstruction of
the self remains possible. Older bodies in performance should project the
richness of all that the body has experienced and embodied.

Within Heddon's chapter, 'Beyond the Self: Autobiography as
Dialogue' (2005), she states that although performance based on artists'
own experiences may be autobiographical, they very rarely just focus on

the self. Critiques who state that autobiographical performance is indulgent, or egotistical, must remember that the personal experiences on which the performance is based is shared with the audience. Indeed, she argues that biographical performance bridges the relationship between performer and audience. Heddon explores four main areas contributing to this dialogue between performers sharing their own experiences and the audience: communicating with the self, discursive performances, engaging the audience, and collaborative practice. She details previous practices informed by personal experiences to inform her thesis. Significantly, for my own performance-based work, is Heddon's example of Tim Miller's productions of *Glory Box* (1999) as an example of how the audience can learn from a performance and then take/make action after the performance which makes a change in society. In *Glory Box,* Miller narrates the story of his partner's deportation to Australia. Miller's relationship with his partner is disregarded in US legislature which does not permit homosexual relationships as a basis for the granting of immigration status. Miller pleads with the audience to allow his partner to stay, providing a political and moral dimension to the work. There are elements of humour and irony as added flavours to the work, which for me, adds to the accessibility of the work to audiences. In *Autobiography and Performance* (2006), Heddon argues that place, history and politics are inextricably connected and embroiled in the performer's self-identity: 'creative practices are always informed by who we are, as subjects embodied in time and space, with our own cultures and histories' (2006: 7).

Similarly, Mike Pearson upholds the notion of experience as essential to performance making. Experiences, combined with memory, nostalgia and self-reflection are integral parts to performance, as he discusses in his text *'In Comes I': Performance, Memory and Landscape* (2006). The title 'In Comes I' is what the text is all about. Pearson becomes an auto-archaeologist, a self-historian and an autobiographical storyteller, who narrates stories about his location and landscape. According to Pearson, performance can be 'a mechanism for enacting the intimate connection between personal biography, social identities and the biography of place' (2006: 17). The performance is a space in which several contexts (self, place, cultural, social) can coexist and be articulated separately and as a whole.

Examples of performance as autoethnography, such as those described briefly above, demonstrate how autobiographical performance is not solely focused on self; rather, the exploration of self equally locates the performer and individual in the social and political worlds interpreted and narrated within the performance. This narration exists in dialogue with the audience. The self tells the story through performance, but the story is constructed and reinterpreted. The historical and political include the understanding of social events: personal and public, and other events which have impacted on the self. And, of course, the audience brings with it a new lens to interpret the piece, where they formulate their own conclusions and take the piece to their own contexts.

In conclusion to this section, although my work is autobiographical and informed by the self, as narrated in my own experiences and reflections, the work is not exclusively self-serving. Autobiographical performance is interdisciplinary, not just in the art form which it expressed, but within the multiple heuristic tools the artist employs to make sense of oneself. The autobiographical performer is a polyglot: interpreting expressions from a variety of previous and current settings and communicating them in a new, original form.

CONCLUSION

Mesearch, as a methodology, is characterised by the triangulation of auto-ethnography, research/practice, and self-hood. The underlying principle of mesearch is to provide clearer accessibility to the nature of self-hood which is a feature of my practice-led work, by using a non-specialised term. Mesearch offers no ambiguity in terms of its self-explorative nature; there is no misunderstanding of the subjective stance of the performance process and output. Yet mesearch is not an indulgent act of solipsism: it is self-critical, self-analytical and reflective. The mesearch paradigm offered in this chapter can serve as a platform for further mesearchers to create work which combines selfhood and art, while adopting mixed, creative methodologies which are connected with their understanding of self and their art.

To consider the affective resonance of such self-recognition, I have chosen features of my archive of collaborative performances and installations that include *Falling Apart at the Seams* (2000, 2006, 2008), *Council House Movie Star* (2012) *and Dying Swans and Dragged Up Dames*[3] (2013, 2014). The three works provide access to my work as I narrate the negotiations of identity, ageing and ability.

NOTES

1. It is with irony, and in the vein of autobiographical telling, that I employ this subtitle. As a school refuser from the age of eleven, I became 'undisciplinable' in the words of my mother and school welfare officer. Dance, in some ways, served to provide a framework of discipline and rigour which I needed.
2. Feminist and, later, queer theory research paradigms support the inclusion of experience and identity as part of the research process. Butler's notion of 'performativity' of gender (1993), the repetition of codified signifiers of masculine/feminine/other can serve as a platform to explore the performativity of self as a complex unity, built up but inseparable from all our identities. Spelman (1988) uses the idea of multiple identities (ethnicity, class, gender, sexuality, race, ability) being pop-beads connected on a chain. I do not believe that, in subjective research, we should 'pop off' certain beads to fit our own research positions; but I do envisage each bead not being the same size, nor having the same import in the telling of self.
3. Initial reflective processes can be read in Edward, M and Newall, H. (2013) 'Dying Swans and Dragged up Dames'. *Animated Community Dance Magazine*. Autumn 2013 issue.
   http://www.communitydance.org.uk/DB/animated-library/dying-swans-and-dragged-up-dames.html?ed=31348.

BIBLIOGRAPHY

Butler, J. (1993) *Bodies That Matter*. London: Routledge.

Campbell, J. and Harbord, J. (Eds.) (2002) *Temporalities, Autobiography and Everyday Life*. New York: Manchester University Press.

David, M. (2003) *Personal and Political: Feminisms, Sociology, and Family Lives*. Stoke on Trent, UK and Sterling, VA: Trentham Books.

Dobie, J F. (2010). 'Heuristic Research: Autoethnography, Immediacy and Self-Reflexivity'. Freeman, J. *Blood, Sweat and Theory*. Oxfordshire: Libri Publishing.

Fisk, A. (2014) *Sex, Sin and Ourselves*. Oregon: Pickwick Publications.

Gómez-Peña, G. (2000) *Dangerous Border Crossers*. Oxon: Routledge.

Heddon, D. (2006). *Autobiography and Performance*. London: Palgrave Macmillan.

Heddon, D. (2005). 'Beyond the Self: Autobiography as Dialogue' in Wallace, C. (Ed.) *Monologues: Theatre, Performance, Subjectivity*. Litteraria Pragensia: Prague. pp. 157–187.

Hiles, D. (2002) 'Narrative and Heuristic Approaches to Transpersonal Research and Practice'. Delivered at the Conference CCPE, London. pp. 1–17.

Jolly, M (2005) 'Speaking Personally, Academically' in *Feminist Theory*, 6(2). pp. 213–220.

Kershaw, B. and Nicholson, H. (2011) *Research Methods in Theatre and Performance*. Edinburgh: Edinburgh University Press.

Laz, C. (1998) 'Act Your Age' in *Sociological Form*, 13(1). pp. 85–97.

Leder, D. (1990) *The Absent Body*. Chicago: University of Chicago Press.

Parker-Starbuck, J. and Mock, R. (2011) 'Researching the Body in Performance' in Kershaw, B. and Nicholson, H. (Eds.) *Research Methods in Theatre Studies*. Edinburgh: Edinburgh University Press.

Pearson, M. (2006) *"In Comes I": Performance, Memory and Landscape*. Exeter: Exeter Press.

Probyn, E. (1993) *Sexing the Self: Gendered Positions in Cultural Studies*. London: Routledge.

Rambo Ronai, C. (1997) 'On Loving and Hating My Mentally Retarded Mother' in *Mental Retardation*, 37. pp. 417–437.

Skeggs, B. (2002) *'Techniques for Telling the Reflexive Self'*, in May, T. (Ed.) *Qualitative Research in Action*, pp. 349–77. London: Sage.

Spelman, E. V. (1988) *Inessential Woman: Problems of Exclusion in Feminist Thought*. Boston: Beacon.

Spry, T. (2001) 'Performing Autoethnography: An Embodied Methodological Praxis' in Nagy Hesse-Biber, S. and Leavy, P. (Eds.), *Emergent Methods in Social Research*. London: Sage. pp. 183–211.

Sullivan, G. (2010) *Art Practice as Research: Inquiry in Visual Arts, Second Edition*. London: Sage.

Thomas, H. (2013) *The Body and Everyday Life*. New York: Routledge.

CHAPTER 5

Falling Apart at the Seams

Abstract This chapter serves as an explorative narrative accompaniment to the dance theatre work, *Falling Apart at the Seams*, choreographed and performed by myself and other invited artists. The chapter begins with a rumination on how performance making processes are not limited to a moment of choreographic conception, but rather all life experiences and creative ideas are ripe for exploration and potential inclusion. In adhering to the mesearch methodology of intertwining art and experience, I use my own narratives of body negotiation and life experiences that contributed to the themes of the work. I focus on age(ing) and embodiment as a cultural and social construct, looking at bodily negotiations and renegotiations.

Keywords Performance • Embodiment • Dance • Ageing • Practice as research • Collaboration

This chapter serves as an explorative narrative accompaniment to the dance theatre work, *Falling Apart at the Seams* (2008), which is the first performance that forms the corpus of three practice-led research investigations. The chapter begins with a rumination on how performance-making processes are not limited to a moment of choreographic conception, but rather all life experiences and creative ideas are ripe for exploration and potential inclusion. Secondly, I engage critically with fragments of diary

© The Author(s) 2018
M. Edward, *Mesearch and the Performing Body*,
https://doi.org/10.1007/978-3-319-69998-1_5

notes from the choreographic roadmap of the performance piece, *Falling Apart at the Seams*. Like all roadmaps, the layout can be complex and messy; the journey can take many routes and many forms; yet only a sample of the journey points are able to form part of this narrative. I consider practical elements and ideas of the performance and its influences. In the third section, in adhering to my mesearch methodology of intertwining art and experience, I explore my own narratives of body negotiation and life experiences that contributed to the themes of the work. The chapter also addresses the research questions: how do I experience age(ing) and embodiment as a cultural and social construct and how does my (maturing) dancing performers' body negotiate and renegotiate age(ing) in performance? Finally, the text concludes with a reflective consideration of the performance and participants.

BEFORE CHOREOGRAPHIC CONCEPTION AND BEYOND

Liz Lerman (2011) uses the term 'hiking the horizontal' to describe how her personal experiences and ideas are incorporated into her performance making. This approach permits a non-hierarchical view of dance as art, as it no longer moves from top to bottom, Lerman describes the hierarchical structure she disavows: 'at the top is art so separate from the rest of culture that its greatness is measured in part by its uselessness [...] At the bottom is art so embedded in its culture that no one thinks to call it art' (2011: xv). In a metaphor similar to a seesaw, in my view this allows for a wider span to view life and art. I view the term 'horizontal' as an entirely fitting lens to view self-in-performance, especially when one considers dance movement and the horizontal layout of most stages or performance spaces. 'Horizontal' gives a sense of time, location and longevity, mixing space and time elements of life and experience. Putting oneself in performance is evidently more than simply add personal life experience to the choreography and stir. Indeed, Lerman notes that her own dance making incorporates 'a whole series of behaviours, practices, and beliefs that I have been working toward for most of my life' (2011: xvi).

In this way, the ideas, themes and choreography which culminated in the work *Falling Apart at the Seams* cannot be defined from a particular starting point which could be neatly attributed to choreographic conception. Rather, within the messiness of life, there are fruits which remain under the skin, in memory and muscle, which are ripe for plucking and inclusion. As I reflect critically on features of the journey of the production for *Falling Apart at the Seams* I try to make tidy the artistic disjointed processes which result in performance pieces. These working processes are discussed in this chapter. What I also offer is an attempt at a chronological narrative and springboard starting points of the performance piece, based on choreographic diary notes and memory.

EXPLORING THE ROADMAP OF *FALLING APART AT THE SEAMS*

In 1999 I began exploring dance and self-age(ing) narratives through practice-led research. This resulted in the early development stages of the now full-length dance theatre work of *Falling Apart at the Seams*.

In making the decision to explore and create work focusing on a self-narrative about dancing and age(ing) from a personal reflexive perspective, I entered into a dialogic negotiation with my own process of ageing. This involved reflecting on and eventually coming to value my maturing performing form and asking myself, 'at what point should I leave the stage? Do I ever need to leave the stage? Why would I ever need to leave the stage?' Exploring how to reply to these rhetorical questions necessitates a degree of self-exposure, and an accompanying vulnerability that results from questioning and challenging cultural expectations of performing your age. On reflection, I suggest that this practical work was a consciousness-raising endeavour. It was through the performance itself that I explored ways in which my career in dance may be challenged through the physical and emotional disruptions of the dancer's premature ageing and how I can perform and write the self back into a visible existence.

Falling Apart at the Seams explored the decline of performers through ageing who had previously attained high, elite levels of athletic physicality (Image 5.1). The early stages of the development of the work consisted of a rehearsal laboratory with dance artist Julia Griffin over a period of four weeks in 1999 and was first presented in 2000 as a 20-minute dance theatre duet performed at the Sudley Theatre in Liverpool, UK. The material was revisited in 2006 and showcased at Dance Cuts (hosted by Ludus Dance) in Lancaster, UK. In 2007 the work was presented throughout the rest of the UK at LEAP Festival (hosted by Merseyside Dance Initiative) in Liverpool, New Moves Dance UK Festival in Worcester, and North Dance Fest (hosted by Shooting Fish Productions) in Grimsby. During 2007 the

Image 5.1   *Falling Apart at the Seams* (Photo: Stuart Rayner)

work was again revisited and culminated in a 70-minute dance theatre performance with the original two dancers. The revised version included a guest appearance by a former Variety octogenarian (June Sands), which I discuss later. This work was then presented at the prestigious British Dance Edition in 2008 and performed several months later at the Rose Theatre in Ormskirk, UK. In the same year the work was discussed on BBC Radio Lancashire and BBC Radio Merseyside and featured on the front cover of the National Campaign for the Arts (NCA) magazine. In the winter of 2011 the material was disseminated in the community arts magazine, *Animated*. My early reflections on the project include the production of a co-written research paper on the project process entitled: 'Temporality of the Dancing Body: Tears, Fears and Ageing Dears', which was selected and delivered at the 2011 international *Making Sense of Pain* conference in Warsaw. The paper explored themes around embodiment of dancing forms, cultural expectations of youthful dancers, the older body as a living archive and themes of how dance needs to move towards the body as opposed to the body having to move towards the dance. Within this paper, I reflected upon and critiqued the processes and performance through memory, including written reflective diary notes and revisiting visual documentation. I was able to re-examine and reflect on the work. My discussion now moves to mobilise elements of my life story, entwined with excerpts from my choreographic notes, diaries, and published material to enable a tidier understanding of the messy life experiences during that period.

MESEARCHING THE CREATIVE PERFORMANCE-MAKING PROCESS

I noted my own experience in the area of dance in 2011, and my reflections were published in *Animated Community Dance Magazine*:

I am not bad for someone nearing 40 but I am sitting (not in a Stannah chair lift), writing this, contemplating a pair of magi-knickers (a must for any ex-practitioner of the Martha Graham technique) after overdosing on multivitamins. This coming of age is unwelcome, perhaps akin to the dancers' menopause: reluctantly undergoing physical and psychological changes, where the aches and pains of my parents' generation now increasingly belong to me. I only need to look into the dance studio mirror to realise I am born naked the rest is just Coal Tar soap. For a dancer, nearing 40, I am considered geriatric. If a ballet dancer must hang up their pointe shoes, at what point does the contemporary dancer wash their feet clean after a final performance?

I came into the dance profession at a later age than the average dancer. When I walked through the dance studio doors at the tender age of twenty, I was asked, 'what do YOU want?' to which I replied, 'well, what you have got?' I knew very little about techniques and was already deemed too old for classical dance training by the ballet 'establishment'. Fortunately, I was given a life line in the way of a university education in dance, live art and drama. I had a natural ability which was quickly recognised and nurtured by enlightened tutors. I was lucky. But my time was limited. (Edward 2011: 22)

In terms of context, it was impossible to leave dance. I was leading a dance programme at a university, yet physically I was shifting from stage to page. Even though dance was certainly the arena in which my theorising, reflections and teaching was grounded, dance was no longer an experiential activity for me. While not experiencing physical movement, I felt dance was therefore something removed from my work. For me, it had always been physical, connecting my mind and body. Obviously, my removal from the studio was due to my own self-awareness and self-consciousness about my own physicality, and my desire not to be (age) exposed. There were times, en route to my desk- or classroom-based sessions where I spent time gazing in studio doors at the athletic, youthful forms, fuelled by passion and stamina as they practised contemporary dance. I had started to become an alien to dance territory. I had no desire to dance beyond my best or to destroy myself physically.

LIFE AND ART

Amidst these personal experiences, life began to emerge into art. As I considered ageing within performance, I started to collaborate with others who were experiencing ageing, or, in my opinion, were old. During this period, I asked British Variety veteran, June Sands (see Image 5.2), to perform together with me. June, an octogenarian, was an example of such a living performance archive. Her career span includes performing the British Music Hall circuit with her father, who was famous for having taught Roy Castle to dance. She had headlined alongside other music hall performers including Old Mother Riley, George Formby, Arthur Askey and Hylda Baker. In her aged years June still maintained a vibrant energy and a strong desire to dance.

During this period of investigation and development, June invigorated me with her physical determination and passion, resulting in a mutual dialogue of shared knowledge, which, in turn, enriched the performance-making process. So rather than focusing on the potentiality of ageing performers to be discriminated against in dance and performance, the work was built around the performer and their abilities—both physical and mental. The process was therefore not one of withstanding arduous rehearsals, but rather exploring abilities and feelings organically: each moment was about new explorations. Considering that bodies mature over time, similarly new production work needs the seeds to be sown, tended to and patience to grow.

Image 5.2 June Sands during her British Variety theatre acts (Photographer unknown)

EMBODIED KNOWLEDGE THROUGH COLLABORATION

It was throughout this process of rich creativity where June's breadth of experience and knowledge motivated me into creating new opportunities. Within the performance-making process, being in dialogue with June demonstrated how the evolution of the ageing performer was part of one's development. There was no point in lamenting what was once embodied, but the task was now to access my own archive of experience and tap into this for other creative outputs. I had to begin exploring myself, and feeling what was comfortable again, and working with June empowered this. Within my choreographic notebook, I noted down something she said which resonated with my own journey:

> when I returned to the studio, I was united with something that was still deep inside but seemed to have been buried alive only to slip back (although slightly changed) onto the bones the moment I started to move. I suppose what we bury alive eventually will come back to surface or even haunt us, if it's strong enough.

Dance making thus explored embodied histories, memories, endurance, and the span of physical knowledge which has developed over one's career. As June shared her vast experience and wisdom with me, I realised the importance of lineage and futurity of sharing this with the next generation of movers. The research and development studio process had allowed me space to delve deeper into the questioning and challenging of how I performed, the language of my body as I matured and how technique may have been held/hosted in my body. What was the core of my physical inscription? What were my core authentic movements? Was there a core identity/authentic movement vocabulary or was I a body of many bodies, a mongrel of previously embodied techniques that had been passed down, nothing more than a body in motion with limited mileage left in the muscles and bones? Here I am reminded of the time I was briefly appointed as Rambert's National UK Touring Animateur. This post involved learning the dance works of Rambert Artistic Director Mark Baldwin and disseminating it throughout the UK. In such a role I was a carrier and communicator of the technique.

DEVELOPING DIFFERENTIATED APPROACHES

After many years of having embodied someone else's dance techniques (mainly those of the American modernist dance pioneers), and although I had my own distinct dance signature, I had started to embark upon a new personal and professional journey. The focus was to explore the lived phenomenology and autobiographical processes of my body, and through this I was able to realign my research interests with my teaching.

During the period of the *Falling Apart at the Seams* tour I had been the successful recipient of a bursary award from the Leverhulme Trust, via Merseyside Dance Initiative, to enable me to participate in a range of dance intensive workshops over a 12-month period. Throughout my career I have been resolutely committed to my ongoing professional development, seeking deeper understandings of the landscape of my discipline and how best to communicate this most effectively. These intensive sessions enabled me to move away from codified dance forms. I began to look deeper into improvisation, contact and release-based[1] workshops, as well as techniques such as Skinner Releasing. During one particular intensive weekend workshop, hosted by dancer and dance maker Charlie Morrissey, I had engaged in dance that involved moving from the pelvis region to better utilise my weight more through space through the aid of the pelvic bone. This was a liberating period for me as the familiar dance techniques I had been practising for many years via the use of my pelvic region were tiring my body and causing aches and a tightening of my thigh muscles. Yet I was in a workshop experiencing some form of dancing freedom from those aches and feelings of being heavy when shifting my weight through space and still acquiring the same performance aesthetic (Image 5.3). I was able to work with existing embodied materials integrated with the more somatic and organic practices.

In direct response to my second research question, *Falling Apart at the Seams* allowed me to engage in a reflective process which acknowledged my own negotiation of age, but more importantly, it allowed me to engage and collaborate with more experienced performers. Age, as a social and cultural product, does not need to be threatening to performance; rather, it enriches it. Throughout the process for this practice piece, I was starting to embark on a journey of self-exploration, and although I did not realise how significant this would feature throughout my practice-led work, it is one which began to provide impetus to create performance which related to self-hood and issues of identity. This provides a simple benchmark from which alternative life experiences can be explored through creative collaboration and artistic development.

As I reflect on this time I see the workshops with Morrissey and the creation of *Falling Apart at the Seams* as a need to readdress embodied techniques and to identify and preserve things that have been and are important to me. In relation to my third research question, which relates

Image 5.3 Demonstrating weight transition floor work to dance undergraduates (Photo: Helen Newall)

to examining body negotiations in performance, each of my practice-led works have led to a reshifting of bodily abilities. Visiting the past can be fruitful, and working with what dance leaves us with is visceral and rich. For me, it was a kind of fine romance one minute and annoyance of possible loss/shift in another. It was an investigation into what might stay that I might resist but feel identified by, what emotional resonances there are with certain dance techniques, people, images and what versions of myself I continue to (re)negotiate. Negotiation ultimately involves change—change of embodied material and patterns—and this can be a complex and an emotional process as it has links to generational investment, familiar bodily narratives, memories, body and geographical histories and a previous physical security that has been available to be drawn upon. It felt similar to losing a close companion that has been on many journeys with me and in some instances on standby. Sometimes the pain of actually letting go in order to establish new relationships with the self can be a cruel realisation and a lengthy emotional and physical journey. This can leave the body in a period of a state of physical flux before it attempts to (re) negotiate.

In my attempt to meet the needs of myself in a better way, I engaged with and developed a range of improvisational work and independent task-based exercises with stimuli that included visuals, props, sound or conceptual dialogues. This way of working encouraged spontaneous action as opposed to pre-decided movements which can often result in shape making and enforced techniques. This resulted in the presentation of a more authentic self in space and increased my well-being. The workshop content focused on pathway scores to encourage spatial awareness; exploring release techniques through sessions that required each of us in the project to become more aware of feelings and dancing from within rather than preoccupied with how we look outside of ourselves. In the dance studio, our backs were turned away from the mirror to enable each performer to experience the somatic impulse from within. I felt this initial creative process enabled a deeper understanding of exploring a sense of self-identity and how we moved through time and space, working with internal sensation and self-reflection. A range of conceptual dialogues were then carefully constructed in these workshops that encouraged connections between conceptual, emotive and the physical 'brains' which eventually became set material for the final production output.

A Space for Negotiating and Renegotiating the Body

Dance is more than a present tense activity: it leaves an imprint within one's body, almost akin to scars. As we evolve as dancers, we do retain these physical memories, where age-related illnesses, such as arthritis, pelvis and hip pain can remind us of our exposure to rigorous technical practices. For me, it was exposure to the Martha Graham technique,[2] which has resulted in significant pain in the pelvis area.

As we age in dance it could be said that the body enters a state of flux, which can be better denoted as a transformational state, where an equilibrium can be restored between new, negotiated abilities and a new style of dance language and movement. In this state, as previous dance forms are rued, they echo in the body's current state. For me, I began to question previous dance forms: were they worth it? My body could no longer accomplish such intense codified and physically demanding techniques, but this became liberating. I no longer had to adhere to notions of an ideal technical dancing body. I was no longer self-policing and engaging in auto-body fascism. I was accommodating my new embodiment, benefiting from the new languages I was exploring throughout workshop processes.

These workshops thus contested previously held notions of repertoire, and how learned techniques were transferred impersonally and inflexibly from dance maker to dancer and which discriminates against the ageing body. There was no longer immediacy of being able to access my previous ability, and I had to negotiate this. The words of Sondra Horton Fraleigh began to resonate within me: 'my dance cannot exist without me, I exist my dance' (1996: xvi).

CONCLUSION

The focus on personal dance and life experience as a catalyst for performance making has characterised my mesearching and performance work. Experience has been a foundational element, even if the focus of relying on subjective experience and memory is more problematic. Engaging in mesearch involves using an approach that does not have to be fixed, or adhered to in any rigid form, but it can be borrowed as an initial concept in which a researcher sets off on a journey of self-exploration. This mesearch approach adopted in my dance investigation was fluid and, unlike established research methodologies, it did not presume the existence of carefully considered theory and hypotheses.

The driving force of *Falling Apart at the Seams* was a recognition of the dance-by expiry date which is inevitable to all performers. The realisation that the techniques and dance forms which had been inscribed in my flesh and bones were not timeless drew me into a search for ageing performers with whom I could collaborate. Through that process, I learnt from my collaborators, embracing the wealth of embodied performance knowledge which fuelled and enriched our collaborations. My own life experience and explorations of new knowledge through effective collaboration with mature movers moved my work forward, and this gave my work a sense of autonomy and a fingerprint of my identity.

My practice followed the narrative method of *autobiography* where I performed my own stories. Autobiography therefore acknowledges the storyteller as sole owner of the narrative. I sought to collaborate with my dance participants in eliciting their stories and actively involve them in my mesearch, offering their first-order narratives, in which 'individuals tell stories about themselves and their own experiences' (Creswell 2013: 150).[3] Effective strategies were developed to build rapport in the studio and to deepen understanding of individual dance embodiments, which have been noted in this chapter. This relationship between myself as mesearcher and my invited dancers is vital, as Creswell notes, 'as researchers collect stories, they negotiate relationships, smooth transitions, and provide ways to be useful to the participants' (2013: 75). Because of this, Creswell states that this is 'a challenging approach to use […] as it takes a keen eye to identify in the source material that gathers the particular stories to capture the individual's experience' (2013: 76). My dance participants formed part of my performance work as I embarked on this journey, but the mesearch paradigm became a main thread of my ongoing studio practice.

NOTES

1. Springboarding from post-modern dance practices improvisation, contact and release-based movement allows the body (and mind) to engage in a more freeing and organic form of dancing.
2. Graham's technique focused on the principal of a contraction and release of muscles. The pelvic girdle (among other body parts) is a strong focal point in Graham classes.
3. Second-order narratives are when researchers 'construct a narrative about other people's experiences' (Creswell 2013: 150).

BIBLIOGRAPHY

Creswell, J. W. (2013) *Qualitative Inquiry and Research Design: Choosing Among Five Approaches*. London: Sage.
Edward, M. (2011) 'More Hip Op than Hip Hop: Temporality of the Dancing Body' *Animated Community Dance Magazine*, Winter 2011 Issue. pp. 22–24. https://www.communitydance.org.uk/DB/animated-library/more-hip-op-than-hip-hop?ed=14075
Horton-Fraleigh, S. (1996) *Dance and the Lived Body*. Pittsburgh: University of Pitsburgh Press.
Lerman, L. (2011) *Hiking the Horizontal*. Middletown, CT: Wesleyan University Press.

CHAPTER 6

Council House Movie Star

Abstract This chapter provides an overview of my interdisciplinary live art and film performance, *Council House Movie Star*. I trace the chronology of the life experiences and ideas which fuelled and were applied to the work, including considering the themes of ageing and drag performance. The cross-disciplinary nature of this art work leads to a critical discussion of queer visibility rooted in discourse on queer theory, and the location of drag in such theorised ideas. I develop strategies for mesearchers to document and incorporate personalised processes into their performance, detailing some of the potential features of what Robin Nelson terms 'liquid knowing' Nelson (*Practice as Research in the Arts*. Hampshire: Palgrave Macmillan, 2014. p. 48).

Keywords Queer • Drag queens • Film • Gender • Fat • Freak

This chapter provides an overview of a second practice-based project, *Council House Movie Star*. This immersive installation launched Liverpool's *Homotopia* festival in 2012. This chapter first traces the chronology of my work which accumulated in the creation of the performance, with a consideration to the themes of ageing and drag performance. Secondly, I consider the cross-disciplinary nature of this art work, including musings on queer visibility rooted in discourse on queer theory, and the location of

© The Author(s) 2018
M. Edward, *Mesearch and the Performing Body*,
https://doi.org/10.1007/978-3-319-69998-1_6

drag in such discourse. The latter section explores the mesearch methods used as part of the creative process. Finally, I conclude by exploring strategies for mesearchers to document and incorporate personalised processes into their performance, detailing some of the potential features of what Robin Nelson terms 'liquid knowing' (2013: 60).

ROADMAPPING *COUNCIL HOUSE MOVIE STAR*

To maintain the metaphor used in the previous chapter to detail the complex journey of attempting to map the relationship between life and art, this first section offers a brief chronology of the development of the piece. *Council House Movie Star* builds on my previous practice-led work where I interrogated the subjective and autobiographical features within my work, for example *The Body's Memory* (1996), *Falling Apart at the Seams* noted in Chap. 5 (2000–2008) and *Flat 6* (2001). Over a period of twenty years, it has become evident that my lived experience has developed to become increasingly significant in terms of being a source of material for the making of performance. I have evolved to be the subject of my own material. During this time, I have started to investigate the relationships between memory, practice and theory and how this can best be revisited, rewritten and reconstructed.

Rooted in outputs which offer a critique of the cultural, social and normative frameworks within which we live, my work encourages others to engage in personal explorations when creating work. The motivation for this mesearch project was due to a personal voyage into myself as an ageing dancer and an exploration of my earlier performing past as a drag queen, and how these identities would transpire in today's cultural climate. In this context, discriminative processes towards ageing are etched into cultural constructs, including constructs such as celebrity, age (in)visibility, anti-ageing, and isolation. Aside from the cultural and social issues surrounding ageing, the physical decline can be just as brutal, as Schwaiger, informed by Featherstone, Hepworth and Turner (1991), states:

> ... the ageing body is conceived as an increasingly inflexible 'mask' which progressively prevents prolific consumption. That is, the physical changes that accompany and mark bodies as they become old, such as wrinkles, sagging skin, osteoarthritis, and so on, prevent people from engaging in the lifestyle of consumption that characterized their youth and middle age. (Schwaiger 2006: 14–15)

Council House Movie Star started as a film inquiry where I invited film-maker and academic Rosa Fong, set designer Olivia du Monceau and videographer and academic Dr Mark Fremaux to explore my practice-led research ideas of what happens when drag queens age, both off-stage and on-stage and how my working-class upbringing could be a site for investigation. Not only did the collaborative film explore the quotidian experiences of the drag life, it also offered a platform for discussing social considerations of the importance of ageing in non-heterosexual contexts and the support structures people create when self-identifying as non-normative. Theoretically, the piece offers further ruminations on the notion of gender as performative (Butler 1993).

The project outputs also included a gallery installation exhibition of a life-size council house that the drag persona Gale Force inhabits. The intention was to capture Gale in various stages of her everyday life (via live performances and an accompanying gallery exhibition of fine art paintings) emphasising both Gale's dragged up body and my naked body depicting fat bare skin and a balding head. By including an exhibition of fine art paintings, I provided distinctive and contrasting media offering various art experiences for the viewer.

My principal aim of this research project was to analyse both critically and creatively the personal and cumulative impact of the ageing experience of the ageing self, with a particular focus on the ageing of the drag persona, and to document the visibility of the off-stage existence of a semi-fictional queer narrative in hetero-saturated existence. The work aimed to capture the cultural interventions of the persona Gale in socially diverse situations, revealing the inner and outer images and emotions of a migrating temporal body, in a state of permanent evolving and becoming.

Within *Council House Movie Star* the primary focus is on the body as a vessel for change: change which, though often unwelcome, is unstoppable. As subjective and reflective as this project is, I acknowledge that there will be no conclusive and affirmative answers. Rather the work documents this journey of change and fluctuating attitudes towards practice as an individual and an artist. In some respects, the self-study is a route to self-enlightenment, moving me away from previous performance practice using codified technical material that may no longer serve a function under my skin. My work explored the ways that the documentation of biography of the performing self can afford a healthier option in resolving and enriching experiences of getting older. *Council House Movie Star* highlights the maturing face and body as it undergoes the ageing process. As a film and immersive performance, the work puts various symptoms of ageing on display. In outward terms, my work offers windows for others to understand their situations in relation to the themes of my work. So, although my work is embedded in 'me', there is certainly the opportunity for others to benefit from my research into the themes or methods I have adopted.

Earlier in my emerging performance art career I studied under the mentorship of Nancy Reilly, one of the original members of the American experimental theatre collective, the Wooster Group. In 1996 I began to explore and appreciate the process of using autobiographical material resulting in a solo project: *The Body's Memory* (1996). It is a subjective turn in my performance work that is played out more explicitly in *Council House Movie Star*.

It was during the mentoring with Reilly, and subsequently performing with the American performance artist Penny Arcade, who were both engaged in subjective projects,[1] that I then became comfortable narrating my own story. Through experience I have come to recognise when it is the right time to tell my story, as 'there is a long time in me between the knowing and the telling' (Paley 1974, cited in Spry 2011: 125). Spry continues, 'you will know when it is time to begin making sense of a confusing or complex experience. You will know when it is time to tell the story' (2011: 124). The film and installation project was just that: the right time. Here lies my complex story: complex in the sense that the work that now makes my artistic life recognisable can, at times, also make it unliveable. It is a practice that creates a bridge from the personal into a performative, a story told of a collective existence as well as a behind-the-door private life where memory, hope and a personal passing are highlighted and uncovered.

The creation and personification of the character Gale allows me to encapsulate autobiographical elements of my childhood memories and familial histories. This also allows these elements to be one step removed from me as an individual as they now belonged to Gale. The persona Gale continues with the monotony of her ageing survival and social existence, while spectators survey her in the setting of her dilapidated council flat accommodation. Here the tragicomic exploration of her day-to-day life unfolds. The viewers become part of the furniture and the set which both defines and imprisons Gale. Although the spectators within the installation do not interact with the actors, they do become voyeurs of this subcultural suburban scenario and immerse themselves in Gale and Mark's personal possessions. I have previously noted elsewhere that 'the challenge lies in the level of (dis)comfort each viewer may feel: how they relate to the personae; what memories, scents and feelings the set may evoke; how they view, and judge Gale Force' (Edward 2014: 149). The exhibition addresses the social and cultural contexts and geographies of spectatorship and how this impacts on the understanding, appreciation, negotiation and experience of ageing for those who have non-heterosexual experiences. As Heaphy (2007) notes:

> It is older gay men, however, who are most likely to tell stories of the implications of age for a sense of 'exclusion' from the scenes and groups that they perceive to make up sexual communities. (2007: 206)

It is these stories of non-heteronormative ageing and queer visibility that are highlighted throughout the project.

QUEER VISIBILITY

The fine art paintings provided a further dimension and lens to the *Council House Movie Star* film and the council house installation. These large art works put forward images of my body ranging from my younger and slimmer teenage years in the 1980s to the much older and fatter dragged up body. The work was painted by Peter Bennett, a professional artist and co-collaborator. Bennett worked from photographic images I had shared. Therefore, there was no real experience of modelling for such work, or to perform for the artist. Bennett painted a variety of pictures and together we selected which ones would complement the gallery space combined with the film and live performance.

The film is 25 minutes in length and documents the personal life of Gale who is a working-class ageing drag queen. Gale appears throughout the film to be isolated yet she is driven by the desire to claw back her former glory days of entertaining. The movie capture and immersive installation performances embrace the idea of age as being a long-time companion, observing changes of a body living in flux. Spectators are exposed to a spectrum of interwoven identities, including queer, ageing, poor, vulnerable, lonely. While I engage with a discussion of the theoretical and methodological underpinnings of the project *Council House Movie*, they are in no way designed to limit the practice. Successful performance is a hybrid of theories, practices, personal explorations and social, political and cultural politics.

Sociologist Brian Heaphy states that 'the issue of ageing in a non-heterosexual context remains remarkably under-studied in sociology'

(2007: 193). Indeed, there appears to be an absence of sociological investigation into ageing among drag queens, an area that itself remains outside the parameters of Heaphy's research. The immersive installation revolved around Gale emphasising her desperate longing for a return to the stage. The work is also informed by social studies through observations and relationships. The unexpected integration of UK 'chavs' (council house and violent) and old-aged pensioners with Gale explored the demarcations of ageing and the integration of a queer fiction juxtaposed against everyday hetero-normal existence. The socio-political overtones included visits from a cast of social workers, Gale and her friends dealing with financial worry and everyday survival among harsh working-class structures. These became part of the substandard stories in which Gale existed. Poverty and challenging perseverance are all by-products for the social and political malaise people live in.

Judith Butler (1990, 1993, 2004) explored how categories of gender are the product of social processes, political governances and cultural ideologies. She notes how gender is far from biological, yet it is socially constructed through repetitions. Thus, what we believe are stable normative concepts of binary gender are actually built on unstable foundations, as repetitions can cease or be ruptured and subverted. Gale subverts the notion of biological realisms to which compulsory sexuality, society, and thus performance, adhere. Gale shows how sex, gender and sexuality is constructed and policed within the context of lower working-class socio-economic structures. Gale promotes the ambiguous value to Butler's performing identities.

The backdrop of social politics and welfare systems in exploring complexities of gender and sexuality is no coincidence. They firmly evoke—and link this performance to—the drag performers on the gay bar circuit whose characters all seemed to spring from low-income, socially deprived, garish and generally tragic backgrounds but whose personalities transcended such limitations. Audiences are invited to observe critically the social milieu that is overtly satirised while being reminded that the performer(s) are actually strong, powerful personalities whom you mock at your own risk (Everett, 2012). This project reveals a creative and academic exploration of queer identities rooted in the sociological endeavour of living realism.

DRAG AS INTERDISCIPLINARY PERFORMANCE ART

What becomes visible in drag is not people, individuals, subjects, or identities, but rather assemblages; indeed those that do not work in any 'doing gender/sexuality/race,' but insist on 'undoing'. (Lorenz 2012: 21)

It is this concept of drag as a queer catalyst because of its taboo nature which can challenge, support and rupture notions of sexuality, gender and age. As a project, *Council House Movie Star* is an investigation into the ageing process in drag performance culture. Drag queens, in rupturing binary gender, fight for acceptance, ultimately finding it in drag clubs, only then to find they are subject to the same norms as any performer and that ageing in this context is unacceptable. Thus, emerges the tragic realisation of attempting to resurrect an embodied art form which has resulted in acceptance (albeit within a safe and structured arena) and achievement for many years, but discovering the disruptions which results in being unable to perform in the same way due to the effects of ageing. For any performing body the ageing process raises new challenges to the physical and mental form, and this investigates the limitations and consequences for drag performers. The film and immersive installation examined and detailed the insecurities of drag performers as they age; advancing research that considers drag queen acceptability and identity through 'homonormativity', (coined by Lisa Duggan (2003), to describe the assimilation of heteronormative ideas into queer cultures and identities).

Drag queens bring the private public in terms of the interplay and relationships with people across the gender spectrum. Such public displays often mask the fact that the ageing drag queen becomes a vulnerable person when the make-up is removed and the sequins are hung up. The unsociable hours of work alongside the stigma attached to the profession can result in difficulties in terms meeting a partner, inequalities in relationships or a rejection from familial and friendship groups. The interdisciplinary nature of my research here offers a visual platform to explore and expose these social, political and cultural issues, thus offering a deeper insight into ageing vulnerability in non-heterosexual contexts. Indeed, if gay culture has often been understood as marginalised, then drag is equally equivocal. Within drag performance there are usually clear demarcated spaces, between drag queen and audience, providing the viewer with a safe distance from the performer. As Maddison notes:

> Drag holds an ambiguous place in gay culture; many of the implications about gender that drag raises are displaced through a voyeuristic celebration of the gowns and the attitude, but drag's status as performance keeps it safely at a distance. (2002: 158)

Council House Movie Star eliminates the 'safe distance' to which Maddison refers with a focus on the improvised encounters and intergenerational, cross-cultural performances of drag in urban and/or unlikely spaces. This interrogates familiar spaces not normally inhabited by drag culture. The work exposes how queer and specifically trans/drag identities in the contemporary era move in relation to and in negotiation with social discourses of ageing which, until now, have remained largely heteronormative.

Hijacked locations across a broad spectrum of social and political settings included: deprived shopping malls; senior citizens' clubs; high couture arenas, busy supermarkets. The performance geography sought to survey and enhance the usually unlikely interactions of physical body politics, street couture, youth culture, senior citizens, drag phenomena and queer avenues. The work crosses 'unspoken' boundaries between each group and explored the temporal gaps that are in existence. Other interventions included Gale's undertaking of community service, hijacking street cleaners, Gale's meals-on-wheels deal for senior citizens and city centre drag races utilising shop mobility scooters. There is a degree of spontaneity in guerrilla performance that can bear fruit depending on the location and the public (Images 6.1 and 6.2).

As drag's position remains ambiguous in gay culture, and on the margins of a heteronormative society, the next section explores further the location of drag in terms of queer and freak discourse.

Queer/Freak Theory

There is no intention to provide a ventriloquist voice to explore the ambiguity of feminised masculinities/masculine femininities through the persona Gale. Indeed, what is explored here include underprivileged and marginalised groups, which fall under the academic umbrella of queer. In social and political terms, the drag queen remains on the margins of society, indeed the heteronormative society discussed by Warner in his pioneering queer text *Fear of a Queer Planet* (1993).

The ageing drag performer is a forceful, powerful and effective narrative of the critique against gendered expectations. Through dragging up with the aid of make-up, clothes and accessories Gale's age can be constructed. Indeed, age in society is often a construct given the billions of pounds people spend in the resistance and even battle against it (through creams, plastic surgery). Gale shifts her ageing time line according to moods, emotions, finances, denial and the company she keeps.

From its roots in feminist and gay/lesbian political activism, queer theory has evolved into an umbrella term to include anyone on the margins

Image 6.1   Gale Force on a deprived shopping estate (Photo: Olivia du Monceau)

of heteronormative society, thus we have 'straight' queers.[2] As encompassing as the umbrella of queer is, and despite Butler's famous assertion that all gender is drag, drag studies has received little attention within queer frameworks, where the focus has been often mobilised by marginalised sexual or gendered identities (lesbian, gay, bisexual, trans, questioning) groups or their allies. Drag is considered an artistic performance of gender as artificial and constructed, rather than a minority non-normative group based on the profession of choice of the members.

Lorenz's investigation of queer theory as a body theory, 'where regulations or exclusions have been applied' (2012: 24) mobilises queer theory

Image 6.2   Gale Force on the film set for *Council House Movie Star* (Photo: Shane Green)

into 'freak' theory. It is Lorenz's exploration of drag as a 'freak' theory that produces an awareness of the possibilities for political and social gains for drag queens. Judiciously juxtaposing the implications of marrying such theory to artistic practice, Lorenz states:

> Theoretical and artistic practice should not be put on the same level. Nonetheless, they do go 'hand in hand' so to speak [...] A theory that is closely tied to artistic methods owes its distance from objectivity, from linear narration, from generalization and from unambiguousness to visual and literary words. (Lorenz 2012: 24)

In 2003 and 2004 I was fortunate to be invited to perform with the American cultural performance icon, and former Warhol film 'star', Penny Arcade in her seminal autobiographical work *Bad Reputation*. Here Arcade openly discusses her sexual experiences, including the violence of rape, and, although bisexual, defies pigeon-holing in terms of a sexual and performative identity. Arcade can be seen as 'otherness' as she is not easily defined in terms of a categorisation, she is totally queer in the way she displaces herself from her heterosexual, staunch, Italian, Catholic upbringing and mainstream heteronormative theatre. Her everyday involvement with drag queens, sex workers, drug addicts and gay men positions her among the societal marginal. It was while working with Arcade I started to question and wonder if queer is positional and ask if queer identities do exist, and are formed through the lived, the embodied and the experiential.

In terms of academia, biblical scholar Deryn Guest considers queer theory as a 'safe option' when compared to radical lesbian and gay theory, and that it was being overly 'applied by trendy straight-identified academics' (2005: 236). I would add to this that queer is often overly applied by middle-class gay youth culture who were reclaiming an insult turned and bandying the term around with little historical insight to a word that had, for many older gay men and women, integrity, history, hardship and memories of unacceptance, intolerance and even violence. It is important to remember the ageing population grew up in a time where it was not as socially accepted to be gay or it was even outlawed, and the stigma attached to sexual preference resulted in dire consequences. That is not to say that we live in idyllic accepting times today, but the gay/lesbian liberation movement has ensured, certainly in the global west, that we live in a society where non-heterosexual and non-cisgendered identities are legally recognised and are moving towards assimilation to straight counterparts.

In terms of the queer space itself, the soundscape of the council flat in *Council House Movie Star* was saturated in iconic music from the 1970s, which could be heard as Gale went about her daily life, not interacting with the spectators. Gale's non-interaction transformed her into a ghost-like figure, disregarding her public in her own nostalgic ignorance. In terms of self-ethics, this lack of interaction with the public also served to respond to concerns about her vulnerability and safety (see also Edward, 2018). Gale did not interact and therefore was unable to hear and respond to any criticism made by the live audience. By placing myself in the space, I acknowledge the vulnerable position I was in as a queer marker, and possible target for homophobic, transphobic or dragphobic comments or assault. Equally, for the audience, they did not need to feel threatened by this larger-than-life persona who dominated the space. In some respects, Gale countered the traditional perception of drag queens who perform on stage, where the audience become recipients of acerbic put-downs. The audience was safe in Gale's disregard. This balance ensured that verbal

Image 6.3 Gale Force on the film set for *Council House Movie Star* (Photo: Shane Green)

exchanges were not given, and Gale was museum-esque in her own personal space, oblivious to the public invasion (Image 6.3).

MESEARCH AND THE CREATIVE PROCESS

As I argued in Chap. 4, there is no neutrality in reflexive mesearch. Both the theme (research) and substance of the study (theoretical knowledge, interpretation and practice-as-research based performance) are intertwined and these elements both challenge and support one another throughout the process.

Throughout the exploration of the creative processes, I mobilised subjective and personalised research explorations. This self is laid bare for others to read in their own personal connections, or to spotlight themes which may be pertinent to their own individual lives. The everyday cultural artefacts have fed their way into set design, props, use of music, costume, location which have all been influenced by my personal upbringing, socialisation and ultimate rebellion against the heteronormative ideal within my working-class town in the north-west of England.

Equally, I am also interested in outcomes from mesearch which focus on an interpretation of the living world as a result of social interactions between performers, explored through reactions to guerrilla interventions. This is an essential underpinning of my site immersive performance worlds, which becomes a focal point on how I 'do things'.

Calás and Smircich discuss 'a reflexivity that constantly assesses the relationship between "knowledge" and "the ways of doing knowledge"' (1992: 240). This, for the performance artist generating practice-led research-based outcomes, and from a personalised research stance, explores how elements relating to ageing and performing are embodied in the performativity. Alvesson and Sköldberg offer a critical examination of the study of the subjective, 'the interpretation of interpretation and the launching of a critical self-exploration of one's own interpretations of empirical material (including its construction)' (2009: 9). The subjective character of *Council House Movie Star* produces reflexive research which exposes and investigates issues like ageing emotions, biographies and relations.

Although my initial process was to look at body image and how my (maturing) performing body negotiates and renegotiates age(ing) in performance the process and post-product dissemination uncovered other questions concerning truth of voice and authorship through the dragging up of Gale. It was during and after the event that this complex scenario of mesearching was contextualised, through the placement of self among a complex web of personas and positions. I started to ask questions about the 'sticky' element of research that is both me and Gale. Where am 'I' among the temporal zones of her drag, my male and female, aged, canvassed, obese body, ageing and fighting for survival in an installation of an imprisoned class structure? While I pivot between also being a male academic who is looking at me through the portrayal of 'her'. This is something that I had not given much thought to during the initial stages of the process.

Within the character of Gale as a focus, I explored and challenged the extent of my own self-exposure in terms of vulnerability in this immersive installation piece. I learned through re-enacting a drag form which I first performed at the age of seventeen, that my drag performance could still draw a gaze—that my drag act was credible as performance in 2012, despite my extensive training in drama, dance and other purist performance arts.

In glimpsing my own physicality, I was struck by the reflection of a much bulkier and older self. My drag has become large and powerful, with a caricature overly large wig, platform shoes and exaggerated accessories. This contrasted my earlier drag experiences where I have been slim, performing glamorous drag (see Farrier 2017). I had morphed from being a 'fishy'[3] queen to a comedy queen. Again, issues of negotiation and renegotiation became part of my process (Image 6.4).

Throughout the work I embarked on a reflective and visual journey of change in order to generate a space for myself which not only accommodated but embraced the maturing performer, moving away from unforgiving youth-saturated performance and social arenas that favour flawless and youthful flesh. Yet, youthfulness was not only present by its absence in Gale. The council estate youth within the piece were all my former students. They had each volunteered to participate in this quasi-biographical piece to gain an insight into the life behind their former tutor and to perform with me.

Image 6.4 Dragging up as Gale Force in *Council House Movie Star* (Photo: Shane Green)

CONCLUSION

As mesearchers we are aware of the challenge and inconsistencies which are present in the evolution of life story and identity work. Dealing with memory and biography in creative terms does not fit to rigid, predetermined and pre-established structures. Therefore, the methodologies used need to be equally adaptable. They need to bend and flex with narrative elements. Mesearch appreciates the treasure of self. Finally, taking mesearch as a methodology, my third performance piece, *Dying Swans and Dragged Up Dames* mobilises visual methods to question ideals of dance performance, using elements of both parody and irony.

NOTES

1. In 1998 I was invited to perform with the Barcelona based dance theatre company Senza Tempo in their world premiere of *Lazurd*. Senza Tempo relished in the embracing of life experiences and their performance projects connected personal stories with broader social and political narrations.
2. See Wittig (1992), Thomas (2000).
3. Within US drag culture, the term 'fishy' is used to denote a hyper-feminised appearance, which one could easily mistake as a biological female.

BIBLIOGRAPHY

Alvesson, M. and Sköldberg, K. (2009) *Reflexive Methodologies: New Vistas for Qualitative Research, Second Edition*. London: Sage.

Butler, J. (2004) *Undoing Gender.* London: Routledge.

Butler, J. (1993) *Bodies That Matter.* London: Routledge.

Butler, J. (1990) *Gender Trouble.* London: Routledge.

Calás, M. and Smircich, L. (1992) 'Rewriting Gender into Organizational Theorizing: Directions from Feminist Perspectives' in Reed, M. and Hughes, M. (Eds.), *Re-thinking Organization: New Directions in Organizational Theory and Analysis.* London: Sage.

Duggan, L. (2003) *The Twilight of Equality: Neoliberalism, Cultural Politics, and the Attack on Democracy.* Boston: Beacon Press.

Edward, M. (2014) 'Council House Movie Star: Que(e)rying the Costume'. Special issue in *Scene*, 2: 1+2, pp. 147–153, https://doi.org/10.1386/scene.7.1-7.147_1

Edward, M. (2018) 'Between Dance and Detention: Ethical Considerations of Mesearch in Performance' in Iphofen, R. and Tolech, M. (Eds.) *The Sage Handbook of Ethics in Qualitative Research.* Sage.

Everett, G. (2012) *Council House Movie Star*. Homotopia Feedback Paper. Unpublished.

Farrier, S. (2017) 'International Influences and Drag: Just a Case of Tucking or Binding?' in *Theatre, Dance and Performance Training*, 8(2). pp. 171–187.

Featherstone, M., Hepworth, M. and Turner, B. (1991) *The Body: Social Processes and Cultural Theory*. London: Sage.

Guest, D. (2005) *When Deborah Met Jael*. London: SCM Press.

Heaphy, B. (2007). 'Sexualities, Gender and Ageing: Resources and Social Change' in *Current Sociology*, 55(2). pp. 193–210.

Lorenz, R. (2012) *Queer Art: A Freak Theory*. Bielefeld: Transcript Verlag.

Maddison, S. (2002) 'Small Towns, Boys and Ivory Towers' in Campbell, J. and Harbord, J. (Eds.) *Temporalities, Autobiography and Everyday Life*. New York: Manchester University Press. pp. 152–168.

Nelson, R. (2013) *Practice as Research in the Arts: Principles, Protocols, Pedagogies, Resistances*. Basingstoke: Palgrave Macmillan.

Schwaiger, E. (2006). 'To Be Forever Young? Towards Reframing Corporeal Subjectivity in Maturity' in *International Journal of Ageing and Later Life*, 1(1). pp. 11–47.

Spry, T. (2011) *Body, Paper, Stage: Writing and Performing Autoethnography*. California: Left Coast Press.

Thomas, C. (2000) *Straight with a Twist*. Chicago: University of Illinois Press.

Warner, M. (1993) *Fear of a Queer Planet*. Minnesota: University of Minnesota.

Wittig, M. (1992) *The Straight Mind and Other Essays*. Boston: Beacon Press.

CHAPTER 7

Dying Swans and Dragged Up Dames

Abstract This chapter explores my practice work with co-creator Professor
Helen Newall, *Dying Swans and Dragged Up Dames* (2013, 2014). The
work consisted of a collection of parodic images which disrupt representations of the pioneers of modern dance and icons of classical ballet: Moira
Shearer, Martha Graham, Rudolf Nureyev, Vaslav Nijinsky, Anna Pavlova. I
engage in theoretical analysis relating to queer theory and camp (Butler,
Bodies That Matter. London: Routledge, 1993; Halberstam, *The Queer
Art of* Failure. North Carolina: Duke University Press, 2011; Sontag,
'Notes on Camp' in *A Susan Sontag Reader*. Harmondsworth: Penguin.
pp. 105–119, 1983). In terms of subjectivity, I explore how my own
maturing body renegotiates both fatness and age, which results in a rejection of the previous codified techniques. I explore the documentation of
the visual images themselves, which offer, arguably, a longer shelf-life than
a performance output to a spectator.

Keywords Camp • Dance • Fat • Parody • Photography • Queer • Low art

Dying Swans and Dragged Up Dames (2013, 2014) consisted of an exhibition of photographs interrogating imagery and authenticity of dance photography as represented in expressions of agility, ability, age and gender.
My interest in encapsulating performance through photography emerged
not only through collaborative experimentation, but also through my own
dissatisfaction of my embodiment. In my previous project, *Council House*

M. Edward, *Mesearch and the Performing Body*,
https://doi.org/10.1007/978-3-319-69998-1_7

75

Movie Star (2012) I had gained weight in order to portray the character of Gale Force, yet because of my own ageing, I had not shifted the weight and began to feel a sense of discomfort in my own flesh. This led to a desire to stay away from performance for a while, at least until I was once again comfortable with my embodiment. The photographic project meant I was no longer visible to a live audience; my audience consisted of just one person, with whom I felt comfortable.

The photographs were a homage to dance legends and re-enactments of renown dance images, where the abilities and aesthetic pleasures of youthfulness on display are displaced by those of me: overweight and in drag. The re-enacted parodic images were produced with a sense of queer play and campness, and indeed, the camp parody reveals an inherent queerness to modern dance.

This work was exhibited in the UK in October 2013 at the Arts Centre in Ormskirk and September 2014 at the Bank Street Gallery in Sheffield. The exhibitions focused on the documentation of a queer dancing body in collaboration with photographer and colleague Professor Helen Newall: *Dying Swans and Dragged Up Dames: A Photographic Exploration of the Ageing Dancer,* as it offered an alternative presentation of traditional images of the icons of modern dance. This both que(e)ried and challenged expectations of performers in terms of gender, ability, agility and aesthetic. The academic enterprise of queering is one which disrupts traditional thinking, and in terms of dance, this project disrupts representations of the pioneers of modern dance. Therefore, queered representations of Moira Shearer, Martha Graham, Rudolf Nureyev, Vaslav Nijinsky, and Anna Pavlova collectively shaped this work.

As the performer in the photographic captures, my frames of reference are not ones which relate to technicalities of photographic capture or the import of images. The theoretical underpinnings relate to the production of the photographs as a form of queer art practice. That said, a consideration of the use of photographs as a form of documenting practice is important to my discussion here.

This chapter has three sections in which the photographic outputs of the project is explored in light of theoretical considerations. Firstly, I reflect on debates within queer theory, such as those located in the scholarship of Judith Butler (1993) and, more recently, Judith Halberstam (2011). My second theoretical analysis explores the notion of camp in performance, principally through the work of Susan Sontag (1983). Significantly, camp and parody become themes which are inextricably linked within this performance piece. Thirdly, in addressing my mesearch paradigm, I delve into my bodily archive to revisit techniques I have not performed for many years, pioneered by these iconic performers. In this, I observe how my maturing body renegotiates both fatness and age in this context which results in a rejection of previous codified techniques. Finally, I explore the documentation of the visual images themselves, which offer, arguably, a longer shelf-life than a performance output to a spectator.

INTRODUCTION: LOW ART AND QUEER FAILURES

Judith Butler explored the inherent notion of queer as a marker of inadequacy and failure: 'the assertion of "queer" will be necessary as a term of affiliation, but it will not fully describe those if purports to represent' (1993: 230). Butler's concern is that once the term 'queer' becomes definable and attributed to a group of individuals or as an adjective to describe cultural or social critiques, the term fails. It fails in its mission to disrupt and disturb because once defined, 'queer' becomes unable to resist normativity. Queer is used as a term to describe disruption to normative ideas, so any description or method applied to it disempowers its significance as a disruptive marker. So, the essence of queer is to remain uncategorisable and to remain resistant to classification and methods. Therefore, practitioners who seek to intersect queer theories with performance-making practices need to recognise these shortcomings. These have been further put under scrutiny by Judith Halberstam in her text *Queer Art of Failure* (2011). Halberstam notes how queer fails, and she looks for some further ways of embracing such failure in the form of mobilising 'low art'. Not only does she offer some examples of this low art, she explores the value in doing so. Her principle is seemingly unpretentious:

> Under certain circumstances failing, losing, forgetting, unmaking, undoing, unbecoming, not knowing may in fact offer more creative, more cooperative, more surprising ways of being in the world. (Halberstam 2011: 2–3)

Within her text, Halberstam's examples of low theory range from children's animation, popular culture, art, film. She notes how such work may result in her not being taken seriously:

> Any book that begins with a quote from *SpongeBob SquarePants* and is motored by wisdom cleaned from *Fantastic Mr Fox*, *Chicken Run* and *Finding Nemo* among other animated guides to life, runs the risk of not being taken seriously. (2011: 6)

Halberstam's goal is to engage in work which is unpretentious as it allows for both creativity and accessibility. She notes the disadvantages of being taken seriously in terms of 'missing out on the chance to be frivolous, promiscuous and irrelevant' (2011: 6) and this critique is levelled principally at the academic community. Of course, critiquing the academic community through academic writing is nothing new, but precisely by engaging with academic rigour and writing continues to give the stature to what is being critiqued. For Halberstam, queer enterprise needs to remove such stature by engaging in the desire for compunction in order not to be taken seriously and rigorously:

> Training of any kind, in fact, […] is about staying in well-lit territories and about knowing exactly which way to go before you set out. Like many others before me, I propose that instead the goal is to lose one's way. (2011: 6)

Therefore, in the spirit of queerly disrupting such compunctions to be credible and rigorous, the intention in *Dying Swans and Dragged Up Dames* was not to mobilise 'low theory' as Halberstam would have it, but to use 'low art' to depict iconic images of pioneers of modern dance, as the early dance modernists and ballet are often considered 'high art'.[1]

CAMP AND PARODY

Camp has become a theoretical component to scholars of queer theory, significantly documented in the publication of *Camp: Queer Aesthetics and the Performing Subject* (Cleto 1999), which includes discursive contributions from Judith Butler and Eve Kosofsky Sedgwick. Predating this volume is Sontag's 1964 essay 'Notes on Camp', which was later published in 1987. Her influence on the 1999 volume is highly noticeable. Aside from the theoretical considerations of camp, two serious contributions to the critique of camp were offered by Mark Booth (1983) and Philip Core (1984), where photography was combined with a witty narrative, and completely camp packaging.

Cleto claims how camp can 'share the contemporary critical stage, the latter being a central issue for "queer theory", one of its partially definitional objects of analysis' (1999: 12). As observed earlier, both Butler and Halberstam are concerned with not attributing a definition to queer, which would hinder its potential for resistance. Cleto here argues for the same on camp, that defining it would universalise it. Indeed, in critical terms, camp becomes a lens with which performance or texts can be read. Camp is a matter of agency, a lens, a way of seeing. Sontag describes it as such:

> [Camp] is one way of seeing the world as an aesthetic phenomenon. That way... is not in terms of beauty but in terms of the degree of artifice, or stylization [...] To emphasize style is to slight content. (1983: 106–107)

In less dense terms, Sontag describes 'the hallmark of camp is the spirit of extravagance. Camp is a woman walking around in a dress made of three million feathers' (1983: 112). Characteristics of camp is exaggeration and parody, which both serve to critique binary constructions of gender in terms of the application of queer theory. I offer a personal rationale for seeking to camp up traditional expectations of dance, as parody of self and traditional normative expectations have been a large feature of my practice.

Mesearch: Revisiting/Reliving Body Materiality and the Pioneers of Modern Dance and Ballet

Dying Swans and Dragged Up Dames presents a living archive of my body, revisiting dance techniques and bringing back to life iconic dance imagery. Within mesearch, one can adopt the position of self-historian, and here I delve into my biography, where I have embodied pure, technical forms of dance pioneered by the early modernist and classical practitioners: an activity which relied on disciplined dedication. Yet this is juxtaposed with a low art form, which I have subsequently embraced in que(e)rying the forms. Combining such mixed methods from my professional archive, a new research output was able to emerge.

The impetus for this project evolved from journeys already documented in Chaps. 5 and 6. Throughout my practice-led mesearch, I have detailed the physical and emotional journey that ageing has on the dancing body. Within *Falling Apart at the Seams*, the process provided a space where I explored the realisation of the ageing performer, both private and on stage. In *Council House Movie Star*, I noted the liminal space created between ageing self and character in terms of performance. This final project, *Dying Swans and Dragged Up Dames*, offers a space where the forms I originally sought to hold onto in my earlier work are disrupted and parodied. The purpose of such disruption, although denoted previously in theoretical terms, was a practical continuation from the characterisation and embodiments I used in *Falling Apart at the Seams* and *Council House Movie Star*. Using self as camp and parody, I was experimenting with dance forms my body still held, combined with my bodily changes in terms of ageing and weight gain. It was a conscious positioning of dance ability with visual representations of forms which are not traditionally seen in dance: the fat, the ageing, the queer(ed).

In terms of the collaborative nature of the project, my colleague Professor Helen Newall was experimenting with the use of photography and photoshop, developing these methods to document performance. Dance performance documented through photographs become a micro-performance, and Helen's concern was one of deconstructing documentation. My work involved deconstructing established perceptions of dance imagery, with ideals which have a culturally expected expiry date and a desired aesthetic.

DOCUMENTATION OF VISUAL IMAGES AS PERFORMANCE

Ruth Holliday notes how a photographic methodology is 'an inherently queer conception' (2000: 503). She claims the use of visual material as a queer exercise in sociological terms, as she links visibility to issues of representation. Holliday extends her own notion of a queer visual methodology by noting how visibility has long been a key and important feature to sexual identity politics and that 'queer subjects are often highly skilled in the communication and interpretation of visual signs' (2000: 517). She continues:

Having been invisible for so long in writing, the media, law and culture more generally, as well as being literally invisible on the bodies of subjects (you can't tell by looking), queer identities have become visibilised through a number of mechanisms. (2000: 517)

Ruth Holliday is informed by Judith Halberstam's suggestion that queer methodologists are almost magpies:

a queer methodology is, in a way, a scavenger methodology that uses different methods to collect and produce information on subjects who have been deliberately or accidentally excluded from traditional studies in human behaviour. (1998: 13)

She also sees the process of using visual imagery as a process of reflexivity, which moves towards the subjective rather than the scientific. This scavenger methodology is one which is entirely appropriate as the props and costumes for the recreation of photographs were haphazardly foraged, as detailed in the following section.

PROCESS AND PLAY

The project was a collaboration with bifurcated research questions. Helen sought to investigate the capture of movement in photography. She looked at the editing of such images, where reality is no longer captured, but later recreated thanks to Photoshop. My work investigated the implications of ageing for dancers and performers. Therefore, as we assembled in the dance studio, I had the contents of my attic stuffed into black bin bags: tights, pointe shoes which had long since been hung up, a Martha Graham-esque black bun-head wig and a long black flowing dress, tutus, white skin-tight trousers, white and black vests and my make-up box. Physically, I had the result of my recent weight gain stuffed between by bone, muscle and skin, which I felt with every movement and costume change. Helen's belongings were much more neatly organised, cameras held in professional cases, battery packs, lighting and other technical accessories. We began to play.

My use of the term 'play' here is not to elide the vast quantity of research which had informed our process, which for me allowed for creative exploration of my body archive in order to create new performance. Not only had I researched the modern technicians I recreated, I also embodied the techniques for which they had become iconic practitioners. My 'play' demonstrated the cumulative impact of knowledge, understanding and analysis which spanned the twenty years of my professional dance career. Yet parody and camp both contain elements of humour, which informed our play. The initial studio practice took ten days of exploration over a six-week period.

The original idea for *Dying Swans and Dragged Up Dames* came about through a call for academic papers and academic posters on age and dance for the 2014 International Tanzkongress of Germany, hosted in Düsseldorf. I discussed with Helen the idea of submitting a poster that would depict ageing. We sketched ideas onto a board and possible re-enactments. Following a range of informal talks, we decided on my re-enacting the iconic dying swan pose made famous by Anna Pavlova and renaming her Angina Pavlova. After the poster was disseminated in Germany both Helen and I wanted to extend the practice investigations to include a range of recognised dance artists, and below I include examples of the exhibited photographs.

Firstly, I present Vaslav Nijinsky as during my undergraduate years I had been interested in him and his role in the 1911 dance work *Le Spectre de la Rose* (Image 7.1)

Second, Helen and I share an interest in old (camp) movies and a Christmas day re-run of *The Red Shoes* (1948) sparked ideas to explore Moira Shearer, as Vicky Page (Image 7.2).

Third, we sought to investigate the dancing stage 'stars' such as Margo Fonteyn in the role of the *Fire Bird* (retitled the *Fired Bird*) and accompanying Fonteyn in the exhibition a series of investigations on Rudolf Nureyev (changed to Rudolf Nearenough), Fonteyn's former dance partner (Images 7.3 and 7.4). Also explored was the contemporary dancer Martha Graham (renamed Arthur Graham) (Image 7.5).

MESEARCH: AGEING AND FAT BODILY RENEGOTIATIONS

In rejecting the hegemonic expectations of the ideal image we have of dancers: young, muscular and slim, I had to negotiate both ageing and fat embodiment while trying to re-enact the dance poses. My intentions were

Image 7.1 Exhibition photo of my re-enactment of Vaslav Nijinsky (Photo: Helen Newall)

reconsidered, as I struggled to maintain my heavy frame en pointe. Having failed to shed the weight I had (semi)intentionally gained for *Council House Movie Star*, I now weighed in at 17 stone. With ageing often comes weight gain (Whitesel 2014) and I could not decide if my knees and feet were straining because of my weight or because of my ageing. I suspect they were inextricably connected. Maybe I was no longer in a position of advocacy for the ageing, fat dancer. In private, I began to realise that dance forms which were beneath the ageing skin and disabling fat, in my muscle and bones, may never surface again. I was not on stage, or performing for an audience. Working with only Helen in the studio space, I was relieved when the clicks were over, after no more than a minute en pointe, and I could rest.

Image 7.2 Exhibition photo of my re-enactment of Moira Shearer (Photo: Helen Newall)

The re-enactments were lit using various lighting states and in some instances natural day lighting captured the moment. An image taken by accident, as Helen was setting up the equipment, became a centre piece in the exhibition (Image 7.6). I felt this image showed my former authentic body/self before it became culturally loaded with the trimmings of specific aesthetic dance forms that had emerged out of a particular period of my life. Those stages of my life saw habit forming dance practices embodied/forced into my flesh and bones and were based on the established expectations for dance students at the time. The weekly Graham technique classes I endured for years resulting in my pelvic girdle and thighs becoming tight and my painful hip rotations through bodily taxing

Image 7.3 Exhibition photo of my re-enactment of Margo Fonteyn (Photo: Helen Newall)

floor exercises. I attended classes in Merce Cunningham technique where I participated in work that focused on limbering workouts for the back and leg extensions. During the many ballet classes that I reluctantly endured as part of my undergraduate studies working on posture and grace and not forgetting the trio dance forms of Doris Humphrey, José Limon and Charles Weidman[2] giving me a deeper sense of weight transition and rebound. Dance scholar and practitioner Jennifer Roche notes 'dancing bodies are formed by the systems they practice' (2015:11) and this was true of my embodied materiality. Although I had not become a dancing 'clone' practitioner I had, however, in my more youthful days, built a bodily agency around those dance languages. These have had a

Image 7.4   Exhibition photo of my re-enactment of Rudolf Nureyev (Photo: Helen Newall)

deep impact through 'the structuring of dancing subjectivities through corporeal practices' (Roche 2015: 11) and an evolving body shaping that had been borne out of dance training and its specific ideological training system.

AGEING VISIBILITY

Dance researcher and former X6 member Emilyn Claid is concerned with the lack of depth in a particular style over many styles. In terms of my own development I studied a range of contemporary dance forms that were eventually amalgamated. In this merger, there was a real sense of

Image 7.5   Exhibition photo of my re-enactment of Martha Graham (Photo: Helen Newall)

understanding the dance in my body and what was required of my body when I assimilated that dancing knowledge through space. Claid states:

> there are so many performance and body-mind techniques available that the dilemma facing contemporary dance is not elitism of a particular system, but the mixture and merging of many. (2006: 140)

Claid's 'dance knowledge' is not merely a cerebral form of knowledge; it is a sensory, felt, knowledge. It involves understanding and embodying dance materials in muscle and bone and determining how best to draw upon the bricolage of movements within the broader range of codified

Image 7.6 Captured by accident while waiting in the studio to commence research on *Dying Swans and Dragged Up Dames*. This image was named 'Blank Canvas' (Photo: Helen Newall)

vocabularies. There was clarity of knowledge transfer from my experience and this integration of forms, I would argue, allows for the evolving of a more idiosyncratic practitioner who is able to draw upon a range of practices that support individuation. It also moves away from 'the process of training through which one's own body becomes imprinted with others' aesthetic visions' (Foster 1995: 113).

It was through experience that it became apparent to me that some older dancers were trying to discard some of their Graham and Cunningham training in favour of something more freeing in their maturing body to accommodate their choreographic work. There are many embodied ways and meanings/multiplicities in the body. Unfortunately, younger dancers tend to have been consumed by classical or conventional movement codes through an institutionalised training habitus. By the time they have reached a certain age in dance there is a need to unpack or re-language ingrained material in order to facilitate a dancer's ongoing potential (as discussed in Chap 5). Motor patterns tend to be in need of renegotiating as we age and there is a need for a shift from corporeal commitments that seem to be working against the skin rather than working with it.

Understanding habit can allow us to 'recognize the body's transformative potential, and its openness to change, including changes in corporeal movement codes' (Schwaiger 2012: 89) and a 'disruption of habitual forms of moving, therefore, can be a means by which the individual's practice is updated to reflect where that person is "at" throughout maturity' (Schwaiger 2012: 89). During *Dying Swans and Dragged Up Dames* I reflected on my current agency and past body materiality and this stirred up deep-dwellings that I had originally been reluctant to put 'out there' for public scrutiny. While I had been researching the effects of age and dancing, what was now becoming apparent was the visible signs of change due to increased bodily fat. I was negotiating and renegotiating two undesirable effects of normative cultural codes within western dance. My focus has been on bodies that tend to be marginalised and, by putting my obese frame on display alongside age(ing), I intended this to be a transformative experience by breaking down cultural normative codes of dance visibility through images of age(ing), queer and fat within dance. As the approach to the creation of the visuals was one which relied on camp and parody, the awareness of the body politics agenda is one which was disrupted, but the seriousness of which may have been diluted through humour.

AGEING, WEIGHT GAIN AND PERFORMANCE

Fat, like ageing, is usually seen as unhealthy and mostly regulated by media and consumerist culture. Media culture reinforces, on a daily basis, the dynamics of slender and youth as a desirable agency. I had long realised that my ageing body had become a non-normative dancing body. This alongside being fat further elided me from the hegemonic social processes of dance visibility. While working on *Dying Swans and Dragged Up Dames* I remained mindful of an avoidance of a pathology of shame and undesirability. Throughout the years, I had been working with the effects of physical interruptions through various ageing physical changes and now I was dealing with fat within dance. The *Dying Swans and Dragged Up Dames* project had resulted in putting my fat dancing body out for bare scrutiny in gallery exhibitions and disseminated. While exploring the ageing dancer theme I offered a visible honesty of fat. Fat visibility is rare in the wider professional dancing community.

However, *Dying Swans and Dragged Up Dames* provided a useful platform from which to explore not only age(ing) dance ability but also a space that resisted the slender proportioned dancing body. As human geographer Robyn Longhurst writes: 'the more that people expose, share, and reflect on experiences of body size and shape, the more it becomes possible to realise that these experiences are wide-ranging' (Longhurst 2005: 17). All non-normative experiences should have a right of place in performance cultures. Performance gives individuals an outlet which means we are not alone; performance is not a solitary practice. Therefore, performance cultures need to engage with the disorderliness which is life, which is often displaced in its representation in non-normative bodies.

Dying Swans and Dragged Up Dames bears witness to the offensiveness of non-normative bodies within dance culture. If one sees ridicule of the fat dancer captured in the photographs, this can be attributed to cultural and societal expectations of the aesthetic values associated with dance, and here, how my body contravened such values. The fat body is seen as out of place within dance, and within a UK context, one only has to remember the 'Roly Polys'[3] as a form of ridicule or incredulity of the heavier performer. In terms of visibility of the fat dancer, the Australian choreographer, Kate Champion has been one to explore the visibility of the fat performance on stage. Thus, the performance *Nothing to Lose* featuring a full cast of plus-sized dancers premiered at the Sydney Festival in 2017.

Embodiment has often been mistaken as a subjective experience, which is aware of itself only. However, embodied subjectivity is relational. Elizabeth Grosz articulates this notion:

> Insofar as I live the body, it is a phenomenon experienced by me and thus provides the very horizon and perspectival point which places me in the world, and makes relations between me, other objects and other subjects possible. (1994: 86)

The dichotomy of the lived body and the physical body is one which has been explored by Merleau-Ponty, who observes how our physical being refers explicitly to the subjective (lived body) and not the objective (mechanical body): 'no [human being] perceives, except on condition of being a self of movement' (Merleau-Ponty 1962: 257). Merleau-Ponty asserts the connection between the mind and body and argues that we are our bodies and they are our 'vehicle(s) for being in the world' (1962: 82). He claims that the body is not merely a mechanical, functioning object. Rather, embodiment relies on both the condition and the context which allows us to experience and give meaning to the world. This acknowledges the body as an essential part of the performing self, thus seeking to transcend the dichotomy of self as subject, versus body as object. Essentially, an embodied approach to both the ageing and fat body is one which ultimately reveals how the body is observed outwardly in relation to the subjective lived body which experiences, feels and emotes. Reflecting on embodiment is not a personal subjective activity, because embodiment acknowledges that it is also being observed. Indeed, Merleau-Ponty observes that 'the body is our general medium for having a world' (1962: 146).

The camera provided the route which enabled me to gain an insight into how one's own appearance and body is visible to others. The image created, facilitated by the technology, became a mirror. Within dance, the use of mirrors in rehearsal spaces offers a direct confrontation with one's own outward appearance. Facing the reality of our bodies, both ageing and in movement is a challenge. Within *Dying Swans and Dragged Up Dames*, I did not view my body as scientifically detached, but I was overcome with the reality of my form, against the backdrop of idealised aesthetic bodies.

CONCLUSION

Dying Swans and Dragged Up Dames is a project that relied on mixed methods in terms of performance (dance, rehearsals, photography) and was fuelled by an insistence on resistance. The project resisted the objectification of athletic, youthful bodies which has been a normative understanding of bodies within performance. Non-normative bodies in terms of those which queer, age or remain aesthetically distinct, have been significantly under-presented within dance. My own process and practices, adhering to the mesearch agenda, required me to make visible my own body in order to challenge hegemonic understandings of dancers. The potential shame and embarrassment which could result from such a piece was masked with camp, parodic elements as iconic performers were reconceptualised with a new focus and a new lens. What emerges from the understanding of the embodied self is the realisation that embodiment can also rely on mirrors, to conceptualise how one is visible to the world. Such visibility in the modern era means that what we see in the mirror can be edited and polished in the form of photographs, which can serve to distort and reshape documentation.

Within this chapter, I have explored my own archive by reframing my past experiences of drag relating to the camp and parody elements of my work, alongside my serious training in ballet and contemporary dance. Both experiences are re-explored through a sense of play, with the objective of refusing objectification. A camp and parodic approach to reframing oneself subverts traditionally upheld body-normative representations in dance. In terms of the mesearch agenda, the subjective stance of research which has underpinned my methods for practice-led research needs equally to be shown to the mirror, and the next chapter focuses on the practicalities of adopting mesearch as a research paradigm. The chapter provides a platform for other mesearchers to be able to discuss their work in relation to their sense of selfhood, identity and life/professional experiences.

Notes

1. Similarly, Matthew Bourne's *Swan Lake* (1995 onwards) disrupted the expectation of the traditional narrative and performance of the ballet piece by using an all-male cast. Such disruption can be aligned to a queering of traditional performance paradigms.
2. Humphrey, Limon and Weidman's techniques utilised weight, flow and focused on a fall and recovery of the dancing body in space.
3. The Roly Polys were a UK-based ensemble of fat dancing females who often made appearances on the Les Dawson Show and other UK variety shows.

Bibliography

Booth, M (1983) *Camp*. London: Quartet Books.
Butler, J. (1993) *Bodies That Matter*. London: Routledge.
Claid, E. (2006) *Yes? No! Maybe... Seductive Ambiguity in Dance*. New York: Routledge.
Cleto, F. (1999) *Camp: Queer Aesthetics and the Performing Subject: A Reader*. Ann Arbor: University of Michigan Press.
Core, P. (1984) *Camp: The Lie That Tells the Truth*. London: Plexus.
Foster, S. (1995) 'Choreographing History' in Carter, A. (Ed.) (1998) *Routledge Dance Studies Reader*. New York: Routledge. [Originally published in Foster, S. (1995) *Choreographing History*. Bloomington: University of Indiana.
Grosz, E. (1994) *Volatile Bodies: Toward a Corporeal Feminism*. Indiana: Indiana University Press.
Halberstam, J. (2011) *The Queer Art of Failure*. North Carolina: Duke University Press.
Halberstam, J. (1998) *Female Masculinity*. Durham: Duke University Press.
Holliday, R. (2000) 'We've Been Framed: Visualising Methodology' in *The Sociological Review*, 48(4). pp. 503–527.

Longhurst, R. (2005) 'Fat Bodies: Developing Geographical Research Agendas' in *Progress in Human Geography*, 29(3). pp. 427–259.

Merleau-Ponty, M. (1962) *Phenomenology of Perception*. London: Routledge and K. Paul.

Roche, J. (2015) *Multiplicity, Embodiment and the Contemporary Dancer*. New York: Palgrave Macmillan.

Schwaiger, E. (2012) *Ageing, Gender, Embodiment and Dance*. Hampshire: Palgrave Macmillan.

Sontag, S. (1983) 'Notes on Camp' in *A Susan Sontag Reader*. Harmondsworth: Penguin. pp. 105–119.

Whitesel, J. (2014) *Fat Gay Men: Girth, Mirth, and the Politics of Stigma*. New York: New York University Press.

CHAPTER 8

Reflections on Mesearch

Abstract Within this final chapter, I reflect on an artist's need to extrapolate elements of self to be able to continue to blend autobiographical performance, and as part of this reflection I observe how mesearch does not merely use a present lens to articulate an understanding or interpretation of the past, but it engages with the hybridity and temporality of the human experience, triangulating the past, present and future selves. This ending chapter considers how mesearch is self-analytical, embodied, creative and a collaborative enterprise which can serve other practitioners and researchers. It is a process which allows the researcher to be self-critical.

Keywords Reflection • Histories • Concluding thoughts • Anecdotes • Memories • Emotions

The writings within this text have allowed me to triangulate my personal histories, my practice-based outputs and my theoretical research in an original blend. I have negotiated my own experience as a performer in relation to age, weight-gain and my emotional response to life's chance cards.

Each of my practice-led projects is underpinned with theoretical blending and personal reflections which have allowed me to address my first research question of exploring ageing and embodiments as social and

© The Author(s) 2018
M. Edward, *Mesearch and the Performing Body*,
https://doi.org/10.1007/978-3-319-69998-1_8

cultural constructs. Within Chap. 5, my discussion of *Falling Apart at the Seams* allowed me to relate to the theme of ageing on a theoretical level by engaging with Liz Lerman's notion of incorporating personal experiences into art forms, as well as demonstrating how work evolves through effective collaboration, and I cite my work with June Sands as an example of knowledge transfer. Yet my work has struck out further than engaging with ageing and social and cultural constructs, as I have equally explored the elements which construct the performances I have created. In Chap. 6, I examined queer theory and freak theory to explore grotesque images of both ageing and non-standard embodiment. In Chap. 7, I explored bodily negotiations which accompany age, such as weight gain, and the process and play elements of combining them into performance.

My work has situated the notion of self among the theoretical frameworks contained in critical discussion of each of my practice-led chapters. In Chap. 4, I set out my me/thods as following the principles of autoethnography, but ensuring that they moved beyond academic engagement and were accessible to wider audiences through the use of a more accessible term. My concern is the reach and impact of my creative practice-led work to non-academic audiences, and this is where the term mesearch and my courting the poetic with the personal seeks to fill that lacuna. Thus far, I have described how mesearch is a more appropriate lexicon to describe the relationship between the researcher and their research, which is less scientific and moves away from traditional research methods. I have discussed how mesearch does not allow for any misunderstandings of its subjective nature and the personal pronoun offers the driving nature of the research a sense of self-hood. In prioritising the importance of self-hood, mesearch does not merely use a present lens to articulate an understanding or interpretation of the past, but that mesearch engages with the hybridity and temporality of the human experience, triangulating the past, present and future selves.

During the process stage of *Falling Apart at the Seams*, June Sands' sharing of her personal histories led to quite an unexpected and emotional response in myself. She shared her lived stories of her relationship with her father, her struggles in life as a performer and her embodied dance material from the British Variety days. As a recipient of such stories, I felt honoured she had shared them with me. Her narratives about her performance career as she entered her maturing years, as well as her considerations on death, meant I found myself an ally to someone else's experience, and her story has impacted on my story. Sands herself died in December 2014.

These shared narratives in the rehearsal studio were not in a neat form which is easily documented in my reflections here, but a sort of emotional osmosis, where I benefited from the sharing of her story and appreciated her collaboration. Vulnerability brings empathy. Selfishness and altruism are set aside when we tell personal stories of hardship and upheaval, thereby empathy becomes part of our connection.

Similarly, in Chap. 6 I discussed *Council House Movie Star*, where I mentored emerging artists and performers who collaborated by visiting Gale in the reconstructed council house. By seeing the development of Gale and the blending of Mark in what was a personal space made public, three former students were able to be part of a mesearch process from which they took elements to produce their own practice. Two of the participants, who appeared in both the film and the council house installation performance, created their own performance-based work linked to their own experiences and identities. Since *Council House Movie Star*, I have seen how the mesearch paradigm has led to other innovative projects. In my current UK higher education institution, I have pioneered the very first level six undergraduate module in drag studies, and the recognition of this module saw mass international responses.[1]

I have noted in Chap. 7 how my participation in *Dying Swans and Dragged Up Dames* was one which led to a wider audience output, but one which I did not need to face. Uncomfortable with my physical condition and lacking in performance confidence, the project put me in a place of vulnerability where the produced images could be critiqued or mocked, but where the production of the images were shown in a safe space. My lack of presence in the gallery spaces meant that there was a degree of self-protection, away from any of the negative critiques I feared would surface.

My own physical vulnerability in *Dying Swans and Dragged Up Dames* meant that within the initial playful stages of the work, the initial shame I experienced through gaining weight and no longer carrying the physical aesthetic which is traditionally normative in dance cultures, meant I used humour—parody and the camp—to mask my inner feelings of vulnerability. I shared the initial images with close friends, and while they drew out the humour, the parody, the queerness of the images, I failed to see through my bursting frame, knowing that I had hidden my weight gain well through the day-to-day clothes I had been masking my body in. It was through exploring these masks that I was able to then engage with the piece on a theoretical level, with my own physical reality staring back at me in each photographic image.

Mesearch involves a process of self-exploration and self-examination, and this leads to work which is critically self-analytic. Through the subjective stance of mesearch, there is the recognition that it is a temporal position which will come to pass. Like performance work itself, mesearch is not timeless. The performing body is temporal. Through the emotions connected to visible vulnerability I have noted throughout my practice work, mesearch challenges the researcher to be transparent.

Within Chap. 6, I used the analogy of looking into a mirror when engaging with creative mesearch, and mirrors ensure one faces up to oneself. Of course, there is no objective truth in this, the mirror can distort because the reflection is only seen by what the mind interprets. Yet, what is seen is still processed, as Custer notes:

> This 'looking into the mirror' requires radical honesty with oneself with the need to be forgiving, compassionate, and understanding, and find meaning from horrific, painful, or troubling events. (Custer 2014: 2)

What makes mesearch inquiries robust is the inherent element of self-analysis and self-critique which it entails. Traditionally, researchers have sought to align themselves to critical theoretical positions which emerge from study and training of the mind. Mesearch engages in a lengthy process of self-scrutiny in which rational theory and reason are not prioritised, but that they are considered alongside other individual responses such as emotions and experiences to inform research. Mesearch is about emotional and experiential engagement as research. By utilising memory and embodied experiences as part of my research methods, I have been able to access a treasure trove of ideas, experiences, feelings, relationships, physical and mental scars, anecdotes, and histories which have all been stitched together in order to engage in a continuous process of creative methods.

Mesearch examines location, position, history, social and cultural experiences. In doing so, it recognises the embodied implications of such experiences. Therefore, mesearch can help to make sense of the work, self and art. Most importantly, mesearch extends the opportunity for others to connect with similar embodied experiences.

In my defence of mesearch, I have articulated how it is not a present activity to view the past, but a continuous present, one which morphs and evolves continuously, as our pasts are reinterpreted and our future hopes change. My practice-led work through mesearch as me/thodology has seen the creation of new performances drawn from my very life narratives.

Throughout, I am fully engaged in how my emotions, memories and personal associations coalesce in ways to form thought and creativity. My practice in *Falling Apart at the Seams, Council House Movie Star* and *Dying Swans and Dragged Up Dames* has deepened my understanding of studio-based research and allowed me to investigate bodies that have moved beyond the physical inscriptions of a stylised language in dance performance and normative idealised concepts of body image. The nature of the work has also allowed me to portray my aged non-standard body, exploring the intersections of age and sexuality, both from a theoretical and experiential perspective. The drive of mesearch enables me to examine the multiple pieces of my life, coming to know and accept my fluid identities, negotiate my changing physical abilities and build resilience and prepare myself for the ever-changing advances of time (see also Edward with Bannon 2017).

Mesearch allows for creative, innovative methods which are accessible in their dissemination to others, and are not clouded in academic ambiguity. The impact and reach of mesearch is essential, as the subjective journey honours individual personal experience and histories, by engaging in a rigorous process of self-criticism and self-analysis. Future mesearchers should build on these beaten tracks by conducting such personal investigations which are then made public.

Throughout the documentation of this work I have negotiated my own emotions in relation to feelings of self-doubt and openness. From an academic perspective, I have engaged, debated, critiqued and discarded theories in ways all post-structuralists do. I have gained four stone in the massive consumption of wine gums I tend to devour while sitting down to write, but I have lost three stone through a recent period of illness.[2] Mesearch means our stories never end. Once this text is documented and archived, the ideas, feelings and theories which are contained here will come to pass, as temporal as they are. However, it is important they are archived for future reference, as other researchers/mesearchers can access the imperfect pathway I have etched out.

Notes

1. See https://www.timeshighereducation.com/news/drag-studies-module-launched-by-edge-hill/2019866.article and http://www.telegraph.co.uk/news/newstopics/howaboutthat/11559490/University-launches-drag-studies-course.html for UK-based coverage.

2. Through contracting a viral infection (while travelling abroad) I have developed myalgic encephalomyelitis (ME) resulting in body-wide pain and cognitive disruption. Thus now having to renegotiate the effects of pain and lack of memory commitment alongside age(ing) and obesity within my performance projects.

BIBLIOGRAPHY

Custer, D. (2014) 'Autoethnography as a Transformative Research Method' in *The Qualitative Report*, 19(21). pp. 1–17.
Edward, M. with Bannon, F. (2017) 'Being in Pieces: Integrating Dance, Identity and Mental Health' in Karkou, V., Oliver, S. and Lycouris, S. (Eds.) *The Oxford Handbook of Dance and Wellbeing*. New York: Oxford University Press.

BIBLIOGRAPHY

Alvesson, M. and Sköldberg, K. (2009) *Reflexive Methodologies: New Vistas for Qualitative Research, Second Edition.* London: Sage.

Amans, D. (2013) *Age and Dancing.* London: Palgrave.

Auslander, P. (2006) 'The Performativity of Performance Documentation' in *A Journal of Performance and Art,* 28 (3). pp. 1–10.

Bateson, C. (2000) *Full Circle Overlapping Lives.* New York: Ballantine Books.

Bauman, Z. (2004) *Identity Conversations with Benedetto Vecchi.* Cambridge: Polity Press.

Booth, M (1983) *Camp.* London: Quartet Books.

Butler, J. (2004) *Undoing Gender.* London: Routledge.

Butler, J. (1993) *Bodies That Matter.* London: Routledge.

Butler, J. (1990) *Gender Trouble.* London: Routledge.

Butler, T. (1989) Memory, History, Culture and the Mind. Oxford: Blackwell.

Boud, D. and Griffin, V. (1987) *Appreciating Adults Learning: From the Learners' Perspective.* London: Kogan Page.

Calás, M. and Smircich, L. (1992) 'Rewriting Gender into Organizational Theorizing: Directions from Feminist Perspectives' in Reed, M. and Hughes, M. (Eds.), *Re-thinking Organization: New Directions in Organizational Theory and Analysis.* London: Sage.

Campbell, J. and Harbord, J. (Eds.) (2002) *Temporalities, Autobiography and Everyday Life.* New York: Manchester University Press.

Claid, E. (2006) *Yes? No! Maybe... Seductive Ambiguity in Dance.* New York: Routledge.

Cleto, F. (1999) *Camp: Queer Aesthetics and the Performing Subject: A Reader.* Ann Arbor: University of Michigan Press.

© The Author(s) 2018   101
M. Edward, *Mesearch and the Performing Body,*
https://doi.org/10.1007/978-3-319-69998-1

Conway, S. and Hockey, J. (1998) 'Resisting the "Mask" of Old Age? The Social Meaning of Lay Health Beliefs in Later Life' *Ageing and Society*, 18(4). pp. 469–497.

Core, P. (1984) *Camp: The Lie That Tells the Truth*. London: Plexus.

Coupland, J. (2013) 'Dance, Ageing and the Mirror: Negotiating Watchability' in *Discourse and Communication*, 7(1). pp. 3–27.

Coupland, J. and Gwyn, R. (2003) *Discourse, the Body and Identity*. London: Palgrave Macmillan.

Creswell, J. W. (2013) *Qualitative Inquiry and Research Design: Choosing Among Five Approaches*. London: Sage.

Custer, D. (2014) 'Autoethnography as a Transformative Research Method' in *The Qualitative Report*, 19(21). pp. 1–17.

David, M. (2003) *Personal and Political: Feminisms, Sociology, and Family Lives*. Stoke on Trent, UK and Sterling, VA: Trentham Books.

Davis, J., Normington, K., Bush-Bailey, J and Bratton, J. (2011) 'Researching Theatre History and Historiography' in Kershaw, B. and Nicholson, H. (Eds.) *Research Methods in Theatre and Performance*. Edinburgh: University of Edinburgh Press.

Dobie, J F. (2010). 'Heuristic Research: Autoethnography, Immediacy and Self-Reflexivity'. Freeman, J. *Blood, Sweat and Theory*. Oxfordshire: Libri Publishing.

Duggan, L. (2003) *The Twilight of Equality: Neoliberalism, Cultural Politics, and the Attack on Democracy*. Boston: Beacon Press.

Early, F. and Lansley, J. (2011) *The Wise Body*. Chicago: Intellect, University of Chicago Press.

Edward, M. (2014a) 'Council House Movie Star: Que(e)rying the Costume'. Special issue in *Scene*, 2: 1+2, pp. 147–153, https://doi.org/10.1386/scene.7.1-7.147_1

Edward, M. (2014b) 'Stop Prancing About: Boys, Dance and the Reflective Glance'. Special issue in *Men Doing (In)Equalities Research*, 470–479. Emerald Group Publishing Limited.

Edward, M (2018) 'Between Dance and Detention: Ethical Considerations of Mesearch in Performance' in Iphofen, R. and Tolech, M. (Eds.) *The Sage Handbook of Ethics in Qualitative Research*. Sage.

Edward, M. with Bannon, F. (2017) 'Being in Pieces: Integrating Dance, Identity and Mental Health' in Karkou, V., Oliver, S. and Lycouris, S. (Eds.) *The Oxford Handbook of Dance and Wellbeing*. New York: Oxford University Press.

Edward, M. and Farrier, S. (forthcoming) 'Doing Me: Researching as Me-searching. Ruminations on Research Methodology in Drag Performance' in Claes, T., Porrovecchio, A. and Reynolds, P. (Eds.) *Methodological and Ethical Issues in Sex and Sexuality Research: Contemporary Essays*. Barbara Buldrich Publishers, Lerverkusen, Germany.

Edward, M. and Newall, H. (2013) *Not With My Body Ya Don't! Ageing Dancers and the Habitus Turn*. Conference Paper, TaPRA, Unpublished.

Edward, M. and Newall, H. (2012) *Temporality of the Performing Body: Tears, Fears and Ageing Dears*. London: ID Press.

Elder, G. H. (1981) 'History and the Life Course' in Betraux, D. (Ed.) Biography and Society: The Life History Approach in the Social Sciences. California: Sage. pp. 77–115.

Farrier, S. (2017) 'International Influences and Drag: Just a Case of Tucking or Binding?' in *Theatre, Dance and Performance Training*, 8(2). pp. 171–187.

Featherstone, M., Hepworth, M. and Turner, B. (1991) *The Body: Social Processes and Cultural Theory*. London: Sage.

Featherstone, M. and Wernick, A. (Eds.) (1995) *Images of Aging: Cultural Representations of Later Life*. London: Routledge.

Fisk, A. (2014) *Sex, Sin and Ourselves*. Oregon: Pickwick Publications.

Foster, S. (1995) 'Choreographing History' in Carter, A. (Ed.) (1998) *Routledge Dance Studies Reader*. New York: Routledge. [Originally published in Foster, S. (1995) *Choreographing History*. Bloomington: University of Indiana.

Gómez-Peña, G. (2000) *Dangerous Border Crossers*. Oxon: Routledge.

Grosz, E. (1994) *Volatile Bodies: Toward a Corporeal Feminism*. Indiana: Indiana University Press.

Guest, D. (2005) *When Deborah Met Jael*. London: SCM Press.

Gullette, M. M. (1999) 'The Other End of the Fashion Cycle' in Woodward, K. (Ed.) Figuring Age: Women, Bodies, Generations. Bloomington: Indiana University Press, pp. 34–57.

Halberstam, J. (2011) *The Queer Art of Failure*. North Carolina: Duke University Press.

Halberstam, J. (1998) *Female Masculinity*. Durham: Duke University Press.

Heaphy, B. (2007). 'Sexualities, Gender and Ageing: Resources and Social Change' in *Current Sociology*, 55(2). pp. 193–210.

Heddon, D. (2006). *Autobiography and Performance*. London: Palgrave Macmillan.

Heddon, D. (2005). 'Beyond the Self: Autobiography as Dialogue' in Wallace, C. (Ed.) *Monologues: Theatre, Performance, Subjectivity*. Litteraria Pragensia: Prague. pp. 157–187.

Hepworth, M. (2004) 'Embodied Agency, Decline and the Masks of Ageing' in Tulle, E. (Ed.) *Old Age and Agency*. New York. Nova Science Publishers.

Hepworth, M. (2003). 'Ageing Bodies: Aged by Culture' in Coupland, J. & Gwyn, R. (Eds.) *Discourse, the Body, and Identity*. New York: Palgrave Macmillan. pp. 80–107.

Hiles, D. (2002) 'Narrative and Heuristic Approaches to Transpersonal Research and Practice'. Delivered at the Conference CCPE, London. pp. 1–17.

Holliday, R. (2000) 'We've Been Framed: Visualising Methodology' in *The Sociological Review*, 48(4). pp. 503–527.

Houston, W. (2011) 'Some Body and No Body: The Body of a Performer' [sic] in Pitches, J. and Popat, S. (Eds.) *Performance Perspectives: A Critical Introduction*. New York: Palgrave Macmillan.

Jolly, M (2005) 'Speaking Personally, Academically' in *Feminist Theory*, 6(2). pp. 213–220.

Kershaw, B. and Nicholson, H. (2011) *Research Methods in Theatre and Performance*. Edinburgh: Edinburgh University Press.

Kohli, M (1981) 'Account, Text, Method' in Bertaux, D. (ed.) *The Life History Approach in the Social Sciences*. California: Sage.

Lawler, S. (2014) *Identity*. Cambridge: Polity Press.

Lawler, S. (2002) 'Narrative in Social Research' in May, T. (Ed.) *Qualitative Research in Action*. London: Sage. pp. 242–58.

Laz, C. (1998) 'Act Your Age' in *Sociological Form*, 13(1). pp. 85–97.

Lee, S. A. (1989). 'Retirement of a Professional Dancer' in *Dance Selected Current Research*, (1). pp. 63–77.

Leder, D. (1990) *The Absent Body*. Chicago: University of Chicago Press.

Lerman, L. (2011) *Hiking the Horizontal*. Middletown, CT: Wesleyan University Press.

Longhurst, R. (2005) 'Fat Bodies: Developing Geographical Research Agendas' in *Progress in Human Geography*, 29(3). pp. 427–259.

Lorenz, R. (2012) *Queer Art: A Freak Theory*. Bielefeld: Transcript Verlag.

Maddison, S. (2002) 'Small Towns, Boys and Ivory Towers' in Campbell, J. and Harbord, J. (Eds.) *Temporalities, Autobiography and Everyday Life*. New York: Manchester University Press. pp. 152–168.

Mason, J. (2002). 'Qualitative Interviewing: Asking, Listening and Interpreting' in May, T. (Ed.) (2002) *Qualitative Research in Action*. London: Sage. pp. 245–47.

Merleau-Ponty, M. (1962) *Phenomenology of Perception*. London: Routledge and K. Paul.

Miller, N. (1991) *Getting Personal: Feminist Occasions and Other Autobiographical Acts*. London: Routledge.

Mooney, R. L. (1957) 'The Researcher Himself' in *Research for Curriculum Improvement, Association for Supervision and Curriculum Development, 1957 Yearbook*. Washington, DC: Association for Supervision and Curriculum Development. pp. 154–187.

Nelson, R. (2014) *Practice as Research in the Arts*. Hampshire: Palgrave Macmillan.

Parker-Starbuck, J. and Mock, R. (2011) 'Researching the Body in Performance' in Kershaw, B. and Nicholson, H. (Eds.) *Research Methods in Theatre Studies*. Edinburgh: Edinburgh University Press.

Pearson, M. (2006) *"In Comes I": Performance, Memory and Landscape*. Exeter: Exeter Press.

Phelan, P. (1993) *Unmarked: The Politics of Performance*. London: Routledge

Phoenix, C. and Sparkes, A. (2008) 'Athletic Body and Ageing in Context: The Narrative Construction of Experienced and Anticipates Selves in Time' in *Journal of Aging Studies,* 22(3). pp. 211–227.

Piccini, A. and Rye, C. (2009) 'Of Fevered Archives and the Quest for Total Documentation' in Allegue, L., Jones, S., Kershaw, B., and Piccini, A. (Eds.) *Practice-as-Research: In Performance and Screen.* New York: Palgrave Macmillan. pp. 34–49.

Probyn, E. (1993) *Sexing the Self: Gendered Positions in Cultural Studies.* London: Routledge.

Rambo Ronai, C. (1997) 'On Loving and Hating My Mentally Retarded Mother' in *Mental Retardation,* 37. pp. 417–437.

Ricœur, P. (1991a) 'Life in Quest of Narrative' (trans. D. Wood) in Wood, D. (Ed.) *On Paul Ricœur: Narrative and Interpretation.* London: Routledge.

Ricœur, P. (1991b) 'Narrative Identity' (trans. D. Wood) in Wood, D. (Ed.) *On Paul Ricœur: Narrative and Interpretation.* London: Routledge.

Roche, J. (2015) *Multiplicity, Embodiment and the Contemporary Dancer.* New York: Palgrave Macmillan.

Schwaiger, E. (2012) *Ageing, Gender, Embodiment and Dance.* Hampshire: Palgrave Macmillan.

Schwaiger, E. (2009) 'Performing Youth: Ageing, Ambiguity and Bodily Integrity' in *Social Identities,* 15(2). pp. 273–287.

Schwaiger, E. (2006). 'To Be Forever Young? Towards Reframing Corporeal Subjectivity in Maturity' in *International Journal of Ageing and Later Life,* 1(1). pp. 11–47.

Schwaiger, E. (2005) 'Performing One's Age: Cultural Constructions of Aging and Embodiment in Western Theatrical Dancers' in *Dance Research Journal,* 37(1). pp. 107–120.

Skeggs, B. (2002) '*Techniques for Telling the Reflexive Self*', in May, T. (Ed.) *Qualitative Research in Action,* pp. 349–77. London: Sage.

Snowber, C. (2002) 'Bodydance: Enfleshing Soulful Inquiry Through Improvisation' in Bagley, C. and Cancienne, M. B. (Eds.) *Dancing the Data.* New York: Peter Lang. pp. 20–37.

Sontag, S. (1983) 'Notes on Camp' in *A Susan Sontag Reader.* Harmondsworth: Penguin. pp. 105–119.

Sparkes, A. (2009) 'Ethnography and the Senses: Challenges and Possibilities' in *Qualitative Research in Sport and Exercise,* 1(1). pp. 21–37.

Spelman, E. V. (1988) *Inessential Woman: Problems of Exclusion in Feminist Thought.* Boston: Beacon.

Spry, T. (2011) *Body, Paper, Stage: Writing and Performing Autoethnography.* California: Left Coast Press.

Spry, T. (2001) '"An Embodied Methodological Praxis'. Performing Autoethnography: An Embodied Praxis" in *Quality Inquiry.* pp. 706–737.

Sullivan, G. (2010) *Art Practice as Research: Inquiry in Visual Arts, Second Edition.* London: Sage.

Thomas, H. (2013) *The Body and Everyday Life.* New York: Routledge.

Thomas, C. (2000) *Straight with a Twist.* Chicago: University of Illinois Press.

Watson, I. (2009) 'An Actor Prepares: Performance as Research (PAR) in the Theatre' in Riley, S. and Hunter, L. (Eds.) *Mapping Landscapes for Performance as Research.* New York: Palgrave Macmillan.

Warner, M. (1993) *Fear of a Queer Planet.* Minnesota: University of Minnesota.

Whitesel, J. (2014) *Fat Gay Men: Girth, Mirth, and the Politics of Stigma.* New York: New York University Press.

Wittig, M. (1992) *The Straight Mind and Other Essays.* Boston: Beacon Press.

Index

© The Author(s) 2018

M. Edward, *Mesearch and the Performing Body*,

https://doi.org/10.1007/978-3-319-69998-1

Printed by Printforce, the Netherlands